Intentional
Grandparenting
with
God's Vision

Larry Hoekman

INTENTIONAL GRANDPARENTING TESTIMONIALS

"Before the class started, I really believed that I was the best grandmother on the planet. However, you have revealed so many new aspects of grandparenting for my consideration. I have truly benefitted, and thus my grandchildren will benefit. God is so good!"

"The seminar really helped me understand the opportunity for influencing my grandchildren for Christ with my role moving from dad to papa. Very enlightening. I especially appreciated the insight on the importance of maintaining a strong relationship with the mother of my grandchildren (my daughter-in-law) when divorce occurs. Thanks so much!"

"I knew I was important, but didn't realize how much influence I have on their lives. It's exciting!"

"For sure, much of this subject matter has not been taught in churches. The Biblical basis has made this class trustworthy."

"I don't have a very good relationship with my son and daughter-in-law, and am now motivated to stay connected with them in any way I can, as it is my responsibility to reach out to my grandchildren."

"The class was so motivational and validating as having purpose as a grandparent. It motivated me not to give up on teens and older grandchildren even though they are a long distance away and give shy responses."

"You have validated many things that I do —and added many great ideas."

"As I prepare for my first grandchild, I found this book to be filled with Biblical teaching and practical wisdom regarding grandparenting. I was especially impacted by how I can honor and support my grandchild's parents!

Before attending Larry's seminar, I was discouraged regarding the communication with my young adult grandchildren. After the seminar, I was encouraged and motivated to regularly touch base with them. And as a result, my oldest recently asked me to join her Mom and her for a weekly zoom Bible Study. So thankful!

This book is dedicated to all Gkids impacted by it,

and especially to my Gkids:

Dakota, Bronson, Autumn, Dekker, and Baylor.

And also to their Grandma, my wife, Linda!

Table of Contents

Introduction

When you consider being a grandparent, which of the following comes to mind?

1. I just take it as it comes; enjoy being with them when I can with a little spoiling along the way.

2. I get involved with their lives as much as I can and attend most, if not all of their activities.

3. I seek ways to leave a positive legacy in their lives and actively attempt to influence them towards God.

Now, more than ever, your role as a Godly grandparent has become increasingly important! You, and quite possibly only you, will be able to touch the hearts of your precious grandchildren and point them to the truth. As the world is rapidly changing and a Biblical worldview is regularly challenged, never before in the history of the U.S. have you been so needed as God's instrument to reach your Gkids for Him!

This book is designed to show you what intentional grandparenting looks like from God's word, and to provide you with practical tools to make that happen. Romans 12:2 tells us that we are not to be conformed to the world's standards (which include grandparenting), but we are to be transformed by the renewing of our minds! I trust you are excited to read this book and have your grandparenting minds transformed by God's plan for you!

Proverbs 29:18a states, *Where there is no vision, the people perish.* This book will give you God's vision for your grandparenting! Yet one can have a very specific vision but may lack the tools to implement that vision. In that case, the vision remains only a dream. The information in the following pages is intended to also provide you with multiple tools to be used with your Gkids and kids. *Intentional Grandparenting with God's Vision* seeks to combine both the vision and the tools for today's grandparents.

In preparing for the seminar and eventual book, I read the few resources available regarding Godly grandparenting. I also engaged in conversations with friends and anyone I came into contact with regarding the impact their 'grandparents' had in their lives. They readily shared the good, the bad, and the indifferent. Also, my wife and my life experiences as educators of young people from 3 to 18 brought us first-hand experiences regarding relationships with children and teens.

The above experiences along with God's input combined to create a seminar presentation we have given to local and out-of-state church groups. Encouraged by the attendees to put the information into a book and study guides, we moved forward. The book begins with God's plan for grandparents and then moves to practical instructions for Godly grandparenting! We believe God will use this information to transform your grandparenting lives!

I trust you'll bring the following attitude while you read: H-O-H. The first H is for Hungry. That you'll have a strong desire to learn all you can to become all God intended you to be as a Godly grandparent. As a Beatitude states, *Blessed are those who hunger and thirst after righteousness, for they shall be filled.*

The 'O' is for being Obedient. There will be some things shared you may disagree with or not implement. BUT if the teaching is directly from God through His word, obedience is the only response! Also, you will sacrifice your time by reading this book, but remember what God said to Samuel, *To obey is better than sacrifice!*

And the last 'H' is for being Humble! We can't do this grandparenting role by ourselves. We must have God's help and depend on Him. For we know, *God is opposed to the proud but gives grace to the humble* and we all need His grace. May God touch your heart and mind as you read.

CHAPTER ONE

Godly Grandparenting 101

Yogi Berra once stated, "If you don't know where you're going, you might wind up somewhere else." We who seek to be Godly grandparents should not end up *somewhere else*. We need to be intentional, proactive grandparents who know where we are going and where better to find direction than from God Himself!

When our life is over, I believe we will sit across from God and have an intimate conversation. Revelation 21:4 states, *God shall wipe away all tears from their eyes.* When we review our lives together and go over areas we may have fallen short, there may be just a few tears. Hence the need for Him to wipe them away!

Specifically regarding grandparenting, God may ask, "How did you do with the instructions I gave you for being a grandparent?" You may not want to read this chapter if you want to excuse yourself with the reply, "What instructions? I didn't know what I was supposed to do." But if your heart's desire is to fulfill the Godly grandparenting role God has designed for you, read on.

11

Grandparents new role. Previous to the 1900's, grandparents usually lived close to their families and interacted regularly with their Gkids. Then as people traveled more and families moved about, the role of grandparents diminished. My grandparents lived fairly close, but I had little interaction with them outside of visiting them on Sundays after church.

Currently, grandparents find themselves in one of four situations, or possibly all of them with different Gkids. The first is that all is well spiritually with your kids and Gkids and reading this should make things even better by you becoming more intentional and proactive. The second is your kids have a nominal spiritual life, and their parental instruction comes more from Dr. Spock than from the Bible. In this instance, it is important for you to model a vibrant walk with Jesus.

A third scenario would be that your kids don't have any relationship with the Lord and are not providing anything spiritual to your Gkids. Here you are to step in that gap and fill in the blank created by your kids. A fourth situation is having your Gkids, and possibly kids, living with you in the same house. These homes, called grand families, present a separate set of challenges and will be addressed later.

No matter what your family is like, God knows your situation! You WILL be planting seeds for future generations. When I plant seeds in my garden, it is done with intentional planning. So should the seeds you plant in the lives of your Gkids as you become the grandparent God intended you to be!

Is God a generational God? Does the Almighty God actually concern Himself with generations and with who begat whom? Has He really been directly involved with who your great, great, grandparents were? Here are Biblical examples demonstrating that God is extremely concerned with your family tree.

The first is this – "Bond, James Bond!" This is possibly the most famous introduction of oneself in the movies and the name Bond became his calling card. So, how did God choose to introduce Himself? In Exodus 3:6 we find the answer. When God was speaking with Moses, He introduced Himself as, *I am the God of Abraham, Isaac, and Jacob.* If He were merely concerned with people knowing His name, God could have stopped with Abraham. Everyone would have known Who He was – YAWEH, the God of Abraham. However, God demonstrated His generational concern by becoming known as the God of multiple generations! He is a generational God!

The second is this – Begat, begat, begat. Those generational lists found in Genesis 5 and 10, Matthew 1 and other places have probably not made anyone's favorite verses list. So, why are they included and even repeated? There must be a reason! One reason would be to demonstrate that God has a very specific plan within every family tree. Lineage is so important to Him that He repeats names within a family tree multiple times! God truly IS a generational God.

Not just in Biblical times, but also right now! Your parents, your grandparents, your children, and especially your grandchildren are not the result of an accidental arrangement of DNA. No, God has created you for a specific role within your family, as He did for those who came before you, and will also do so regarding those coming after you!

ACTION PLANS: Each chapter will conclude with a few questions or thoughts designed for you to write what you are proactively and intentionally going to be doing as you seek to make Godly impressions on your Gkids' hearts! Some will be very short, while others will require more.

ACTION PLAN – CHAPTER ONE

What has your approach to being a grandparent been previous to now?

Say a prayer that God opens your heart and mind to consider ways to become the Godly grandparent He has designed you to be.

CHAPTER TWO

God's Plan For The Family

This is a long chapter, but so very foundational to understand God's vision for us grandparents. So if God is a generational God, it makes complete sense that He has a very specific plan for each family within those generations of begats! This plan will be divided into four parts. First His plan for humanity; then the role of families; next His desire for individual families, and finally and most importantly for you as you read this – His very specific plan for grandparents!

First, God's plan for all of humanity. This plan is clearly stated in both the Old and New Testaments. When Jesus was asked which was the greatest commandment, He responded with this in Matthew 22:37, *You are to love the Lord your God with all of your heart, and with all of your soul, and with all of your mind.*

By speaking these words, Jesus was quoting from The Shema, Judaism's declaration of faith in one God, found in Deuteronomy 6:4-9. In verse 6 it reads, *You shall love the Lord your God with all of your heart, and with all your soul, and with all your might.* So God's plan for humanity is clearly stated, and restated by Jesus! A very specific plan!

A quick question – how are you doing in this area? Before you read on, if you have lost that first love, take some time and recommit your love to Him and always seek to follow Jesus' command to love the Lord your God with all of your heart, soul, mind, and strength! Your personal relationship with Jesus will be a primary factor as you seek to be a Godly influence in your Gkids' lives. If needed, stop right now and commit fully to God's call on your life.

Second, what about families? While shopping in an antiques and more store, I saw an inscription on a piece of wood which read, 'Family: Nature's Greatest Invention.' NOT!!! The natural world of plants has little if any family structure! Later we will talk about the minimal family life of animals, so it is a big 'no' on nature's role in the creation of families. God did! Family is God's greatest invention, not nature's.

But is there a reason God appears to have created only one family? And why do our children live within the family unit so much longer than animals?

It appears that God created multiples of the same type of animal, i.e. not just two German Shepherds, but many. And it was the same with vegetation, as He didn't just create one carrot. Yet He chose to create only one family unit. For God to create ONE singular family tree, families had to start with one family. That way, all of us are united by physical procreation begun by Adam and Eve. In Genesis 1 we were commanded to be fruitful and multiply. For obvious reasons, this may have been Adam's favorite commandment!

And just as important within all families, parents were to spiritually and morally procreate as well. Starting with the first family, we were to teach our families that most important commandment regarding loving God with all of our hearts. If successful and each family followed His initial plan, the one human race would grow in number, and in the knowledge of the Almighty. And God called that plan, GOOD! The physical procreation plan went extremely well as we now have over seven billion humans on this planet.

The second part of His plan ran into a bit of a problem called free will. Our use of God's gift of free will has struggled since that first family where it soon reared its ugly head. Its self-centered philosophy of choosing to behave in whatever fashion we want sadly expressed itself within the first family unit and has never stopped wreaking havoc within our families and the family of God. The misuse of free will stymied the spiritual aspect of God's plan from the beginning. Instead, the family unit can only try to impart God's commands to our children and grandchildren, as each person is allowed to freely respond - follow God or follow self. Later in the book, you will read your specific role as grandparents regarding your influence in the lives of your Gkids.

Have you ever wondered why animals only raise their offspring for a short time, but we humans are gifted with our children for 18 years, or until they sort of become adults? And many of our children hang around even longer. Why do fish serve no parental time? Why do almost all animals abandon any parental responsibilities before their 'kids' are only 2 years old? And those who stay longer are often with Mom alone. So, that begs the question, *why did God create human families to care for their young for so long?*

This extended time of parenting is because the family unit is to be the primary method of learning about God, learning to trust in Him, and developing a relationship with the Father, Son, and Holy Spirit. I completely agree with Rob Rienow, who wrote in Visionary Parenting that God's plan for families is for the family unit to evangelize and disciple their children. For animals, God gave them an instinctual guidebook to follow. For people, God's plan was not instinctual, but one which was to be taught from one generation to the next!

So how are families doing? Statistics tell us why evangelizing the children within the family is so vital in God's plan. It is reported that among adult followers of Christ, 77% came to Christ before they were 18. And where are people under 18? Within the family unit! This is when the harvest is ripe, and it is the responsibility of the family to do whatever they can to bring those precious children to a saving knowledge of Jesus!

However, studies also state that up to 70% of adults who went to youth group as a young person no longer attend church, and their commitment to the Lord has been minimized. So it's not a simple matter of getting children to say the sinner's prayer and we've done our job. No, we are to teach, instruct, and disciple them so that they will not become part of that 70%!

In summary, families have been given adequate time to do everything they can to encourage their children to receive the Lord, and then follow that with Godly input and instruction giving them a strong foundation in Christ when they leave home! A vital responsibility.

What about the individual family unit? Does God have an intentional plan for each family tree, or do the branches and leaves come as simply a physical process of having children in a haphazard fashion guided only by DNA? No, God's plan for each family is intentional and purposeful!

This part of the plan directly involves you! And it is for ALL of you. As an example, one family stopped going to my Grandparenting seminar after hearing about God's specific plan for the family. When I asked why, they stated that because their family tree was much more like a family bush. There was so much dysfunction, they believed they were outside of God's plan. As a result, in following seminars I've made sure to address those who might feel that way. God foreknew how each of your family situations would be and STILL had an intentional and purposeful place for YOU within the chaos or whatever your family tree may look like. I'll repeat this often! Grandparent – you are an integral part of God's plan for your family; regardless of its dysfunction!

God hasn't hidden His intentions from us. In Psalm 100:3 it reads, *It is He that has made us and not we ourselves.* God is the One responsible for our existence. Sure, as parents we played a role in the process. But any couple who had difficulty becoming pregnant like my wife and me, knows that it is not a matter of inserting Tab A into Slot B and having a child. For us, months and months of trying resulted in nothing. Then one month Linda was pregnant even though we weren't doing anything differently. No, we must recognize this fact: God has made each and every child!

Just how specific was He when we were created? I've read that given the various eggs within the Mom and the over 500 billion sperm a male produces over their lifetime, potentially one sexual encounter has the mathematical chance of producing 64 trillion different humans. And out came you! Those numbers are a bit mind-boggling, but let's assume that you had a 1:64,000,000,000,000 of being you and here you are. Did God play a role in that, or did our DNA come together by mere happenstance? Again, Psalms has the answer!

Psalm 139:13 tells us, *For You formed my inward parts; You wove me in my mother's womb.* God used this terminology at that time because had the Psalmist wrote that God pieced together our DNA, none of those readers would have had a clue what was being talked about. However, today we know that we are a result of an intricate weaving together of our DNA, and who did the weaving – God Himself! I find this to be an exciting confirmation of Psalm 139. When I look at a pictorial representation of our DNA, it looks to me like someone wove together a ribbon-like cloth. And that weaver is God!

Therefore, it logically follows that if God wove you together, He also did the same for everyone in your individual family. Your parents, grandparents, great grandparents, children, **grandchildren,** great-grandchildren, and on and on!

God's perfect plan. Because one of God's characteristics is foreknowledge (a concept I can't quite wrap my head around), He could be extremely intentional as to how He created our family tree. Any of you who have raised more than one child know that each one was very unique in multiple ways. And when God designed what we now call our *nature,* He was well aware of what our nurture was going to be. He also knew what our life experiences would be. And on top of that, for Christ-followers, He knew what gifts He would bless us with. And He knew exactly who would be our grandchildren. His creation of us was intentionally and purposefully done so that we would fit perfectly within our individual family unit. Not that we would be the perfect family, but that each of us would be His perfect instrument for His use within whatever situation you find yourself – right here; right now!

At this point, you may feel like you're not the perfect fit in your role as a grandparent. You're right; you're not. BUT with God partnering with you, you ARE!

Yes, He made you perfectly suited to be His partner to grandparent each of your grandchildren! Sounds crazy, but it's true! When my kids were growing up, it used to take me back a bit when one of their friends might say something like, "My Dad is the best Dad in the whole world." I thought (but didn't say!), "No, I'm the best Dad in the world, so yours would have to be no better than #2!" Now I realize that in God's perfect plan, it is His intent that each one of us is the perfect grandparent to the grandchildren He created for us to minister to!

This plan was specifically and intentionally orchestrated by Almighty God for a very specific purpose! And that purpose is that all family members (you) have been uniquely designed to fulfill the exact role God has for them (you) within their (your) family!! This is so important I'll repeat it – the purpose is that family members have been uniquely designed to fulfill the exact role God has for them within their family!

Grandparents, you are special! Yes, you can stand in front of the grandparenting mirror, look at yourself, and humbly state, "I am special! I'm not just getting older and closer to going to heaven. God's eternal plan for me is to fill that 'special' place in the life of my grandchildren." In THIS place, at THIS time, for THIS purpose – to be the best grandparent in the whole world! That IS God's vision for you as a grandparent!

So **grandparent,** did God leave any specific instructions for you regarding grandparenting? YES, and it is way more detailed than you might think. No, the Christian bookstores don't have a grandparenting section. And even if you've gone to church your whole life like my wife and I have, you've probably heard very little teaching on being a godly grandparent. So you might assume there is little or nothing in the Bible to help you in your role as a grandparent. However, God's word has NOT left us to struggle on our own and grandparent from a secular worldview. God has told us what to do, what to say, why we are to do and say those things, and much more.

Read on!

ACTION PLAN - CHAPTER TWO

On a 1 -10, where would you rate yourself regarding loving God with all your heart, soul, and mind? If it's not a 10, commit to loving Him more!

Looking back on your parenting, how could you, if at all, improve in helping to evangelize and disciple your Gkids?

Do you agree that God has intentionally and purposefully placed you as the perfect grandparent for each of your Gkids? What difference does that make to your role as grandparent?

CHAPTER THREE

God's Instructions For Grandparents

First, I'll list verses which directly address your role as a Godly grandparent, and then I'll expand on each. Later, I'll refer to other verses which indirectly refer to grandparenting.

Deuteronomy 4:9b,10: God speaking – *"Make the things I have done for you known to your sons and your children's children. Remember the day you stood before the Lord your God at Horeb, when the Lord said to Moses, 'Assemble the people to Me, that I may let them hear My words so they may learn to fear Me all the days they live on the earth, and that they may teach their children.'"*

Deuteronomy 6:1,2: *These are the commandments and statues that you might do them . . . so that your grandchildren will fear the Lord and keep His commandments as well.*

Proverbs 17:6: *Grandchildren are the crown of grandparents*

Proverbs 13:22: *A good grandparent leaves an inheritance to their grandchildren.*

II Timothy 1:5: *I, Paul, am reminded of the sincere faith within you, which first dwelt in your grand-mother.*

Psalm 103:17: *But the loving-kindness of the Lord is from everlasting to everlasting on those who fear Him, and His righteousness to grandchildren.*

Before I expand on these verses, I need to interject a thought referred to earlier about our life in heaven. I call it our heavenly table talk where we will sit down with God and talk about our earthly lives. At this time He'll review the various aspects of our lives, and one of those could be this question, "So, how did you do in your role of grandparent for those precious lives I entrusted you with?" Our response might include teaching them how to fish; going to their games or performances; babysitting them; spoiling them and more. Then God may say, "No, I meant how did you do with the guidance I gave you in My word regarding being a Godly grandparent?"

Here we may become a bit stuck, as many of us are unaware of what He desires for us in this area. Earlier we shared that this might be a time of tears, but once we begin intentionally applying His word, this table talk about grandparenting should be a joy-filled part of that conversation!

The first verses from Deuteronomy are very specific as to what grandparents are to say and why they are to say those things! Deuteronomy 4:9b,10: God speaking – "*Make the things I have done for you known to your sons and your children's children. Remember the day you stood before the Lord your God at Horeb, when the Lord said to Moses, 'Assemble the people to Me, that I may let them hear my words so they may learn to fear Me all the days they live on the earth, and that they may teach their children.'*"

27

The modern world combines electricity and technology so that there is almost any form of entertainment at our fingertips at any time. This is restricting our family time making the oral sharing of family history almost history. But God wants us, as Godly grandparents, to resurrect this! These verses tell us we ARE to tell our Gkids what God has done for us! Not what we're doing for Him, but what He is doing in and through our lives. Many people, like phony TV preachers, can fake what they are doing for God, but it is hard to be deceptive when telling them what God is doing in your life.

Storytelling by sharing with our Gkids the many ways God has intervened in our lives is not a suggestion. The first word, "Make," is a command word! This directive from God is for a good reason and that reason is also spelled out - so they (Gkids) may learn to fear Me all the days they live on the earth. The word fear is repeated in the next Deuteronomy grandparenting verses, so I'll address it now. Psalm 130:3,4 tells us, *If You Lord remembered everyone's sins, who could stand? But with You there is FORGIVENESS, so that we may* **fear** *You.* So the word translated 'fear' does not mean that we share what God has done in our lives so that our Gkids would be afraid of Him. No, it means that they would learn to respect, honor, reverence, and be in awe of our God! I can't emphasize this enough!

We can't force our Gkids to love God, but like what is illustrated in the parable of the Sower and the Seed, we are to help make fertile soil within the hearts of our Gkids, to make it easier for them to come to Christ. My wife and I visited the Billy Graham Library, and I was struck by a comment from his wife, Ruth. She was talking about her parents and said that not only were they missionaries, but they also lived the Christian life at home in such a way it made it EASY for her to believe in Jesus. What a great description of our role as Godly grandparents! One way we are to do that is by sharing our history in terms of what God has done in our lives.

Miscarriages have been part of our extended families' lives and our own. Looking back, we realized we did my daughter a disservice by not following God's command to share what He had done in our lives after our miscarriages. We knew how God had taken care of us through those times, but didn't purpose in our hearts to share that. When my daughter experienced her own miscarriage, she did not know our history of God's provision. Therefore she basically had to go through this experience without the wisdom and perspective gained from us. It was only after the fact that we shared how God took care of us, and it provided some help. Sadly, we believe if we had been proactive instead of reactive, she would have had a much easier time.

ACTION PLAN – CHAPTER THREE

What is your initial response to the totality of verses directly related to grandparents?

How are you going to *make things God has done for you* known to your Gkids?

CHAPTER FOUR

More Grandparenting Verses

Now for the second set of verses found in Deuteronomy – chapter 6:1,2: *These are the command-ments and statues that you might do them . . . so that your grandchildren will fear the Lord and keep His commandments as well.* It's simply said, but a bit harder to do! God tells us to keep His commandments, and to do it with a purpose – to impact the hearts and minds of our Gkids so they will fear Him. And there's that word 'fear' again! Fear – to be in awe of, to reverence, to respect, and to honor.

These verses state directly what we are to do and why to do it! Very specific instructions.

So fellow grandparents, God has told us what to say; what to do; and why to say and do them! In your role as a parent, I'm sure that if you told your kids what to say and what to do, you would consider those pretty explicit instructions, and you would expect them to follow those instructions! SO DOES GOD!

Proverbs 17:6: *Grandchildren are the crown of grandparents.* At first, I thought this to be something like a bragging point. You have probably all experienced walking your baby grandchild, and a passersby oohing and aahing over them while hardly paying any attention to you! They were our delight – our crown. But after considering this more and specifically focusing on the word crown within the context of the time the verses were written, I ended up with a far different conclusion.

One's crown indicated one's position - a king, queen, or any other position of royalty. So, our grandchildren ARE our position and role in this our latter stage of life! As the position of king indicated by the king's crown required certain responsibilities, so our position as grandparent indicates our own set of responsibilities! All done out of love for them and in obedience to the Lord!

Proverbs 13:22: *A good grandparent leaves an inheritance to their grandchildren.* We know this inheritance is not money, as you can easily fill in this blank –'the love of money is the root of all _____.' So God would not tell us to leave our Gkids a legacy whose focus is on money. The word inheritance would better be understood as 'impression.' As Godly grandparents, we are to definitely leave a Godly impression on the hearts and minds of our Gkids. There is much more on this topic during the chapter about our legacy.

II Timothy 1:5: *I, Paul, am reminded of the sincere faith within you, which first dwelt in your grandmother.* Earlier we shared how God is a generational God, and this verse confirms it. God, speaking through Paul, wanted to remind us that leaving a spiritual heritage is extremely important to Him, and something we should aspire to continually. And if you are the first in your family to be a Christ-follower, this verse could someday be written about YOU!

Psalm 103:17: *But the loving-kindness of the Lord is from everlasting to everlasting on those who fear Him, and His righteousness to grandchildren.* God wants to extend righteousness, or the right way of living, to our grandchildren, and who is the only one who can extend something to grand-children? Grandparents! Parents to their kids; grandparents to their Gkids. If God is to use us to show righteousness to our Gkids, then we should now have a favorite Beatitude – Matthew 5:6. *"Blessed are those who hunger and thirst after righteousness, for they shall be filled."* There is no better way to input something into someone else than to overflow with it. So, as Godly grandparents, we should be hungering and thirsting after righteousness, so we can give what God wants us to give to our Gkids, by overflowing with righteousness! May that be our desire each and every day.

These verses give us God's direct vision for our role as grandparents. There are a lot of other great secular things we can and should do in this role, but God's calling on our lives is clear. The question is, how are we now going to respond to that calling? Remember the heavenly table talk with God? By choosing our role as grandparents as our number one ministry, we can fulfill God's plan for the family and have a wonderful table talk!

God has chosen to Partner with us; He has Prepared us via our nature, nurture, life experiences, and gifting; He has a grandparenting Plan specifically for us; and that plan has a very detailed Purpose. As Godly grandparents, we are Partnered, Prepared, given a Plan, and have a Purpose! May we all rise up to fulfill God's vision for us!

ACTION PLAN – CHAPTER FOUR

List 3 to 5 things you are going to do differently now that you are fully aware of God's instructions for grandparents.

When you have your table talk with God in heaven, how would you like Him to view your role as a Godly grandparent?

Which verse in this chapter is the most meaningful to you and why?

CHAPTER FIVE

Impressing The Hearts Of Our Gkids

This phrase will be repeated a number of times - 'to impress the hearts of your Gkids.' Remember God's plan for humanity was for us to 'love Him with all of our heart, soul, mind, and strength,' and the first one on the list is our heart! We should be focusing our remaining time on the number one thing in life for our Gkids – for them to love the Lord with all their hearts! It is their heart, not their mind (how well they do in school) or their strength (sports) that is God's most important priority. And it should be ours as well. The others should also be addressed; however, God is calling us as Godly grandparents to make a purposeful and intentional impression on the 'hearts' of each one of our Gkids!

I asked a fellow Christ-following ceramics teacher to help me illustrate the point of being purposeful and intentional. She took a lump of clay and made a work of art. This piece was fashioned without her being intentional or purposeful, as she just made random artistic impressions on the clay.

This is what she came up with:

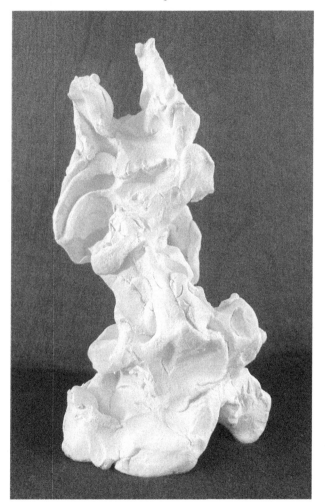

For the second one, I used a ceramic piece which was done in a very purposeful and intentional way. This was the result:

What a difference purposefulness and intentionality made in the final product! And the same can be true for us, as it is the goal of this book to give you a specific direction to take in regards to your role as a Godly grandparent. We can't control the final product like my ceramics teaching friend did, but we can control how we respond to God's vision for our grandparenting. Let the adventure begin!

First, a bit of encouragement. In the introduction, I referred to feeling guilty at a parenting conference as to my lack of truly achieving the maximum in my role as a Godly parent. This prompted me to start teaching workshops on grandparenting. At this point you might be feeling a bit guilty yourself, so I want to encourage you before you go on. Philippians 3:13, 14 is key to this and will also be used at the very end of the book. Paul is reviewing his past and then writes, *"But this one thing I do; forgetting what lies behind and reaching forward to what lies ahead, I press on toward the goal for the prize of the upward call of God in Christ Jesus."*

Be encouraged! Focus on what lies ahead. The past cannot be changed, but the future can be one of always reaching forward to what lies ahead! Remember grandparents, God has kept you alive this long for a reason and needs you to partner with Him in the FUTURE to impress your Gkids' hearts! It's never too late to do the right thing.

How do we start impressing their hearts? You can begin right now. We live in the best time in history to stay in contact with our Gkids no matter where they live. There are so many ways to connect, and we should use the method they prefer. For most young people, that appears to be texting. My fingers are big and texting is not fun – UNTIL I began to talk to text. I need to proof-read, but it is now so much faster and easier.

No excuses! At your table talk with God, you don't want to try to defend why you didn't contact your God-given Gkids. If you don't want to use texting, Facetime, Skype, Email, Twitter, be a Facebook friend (maybe too much info there), and the good old phone are all ways for you to start making a regular connection with them. Also, don't ignore snail mail. Because it is received so infrequently in the lives of young people, it has become that much more special. Write them a note and mail it – maybe today! And within that note, you may want to share how you're reading a grandparenting book and how God is working in your life to become a better grandparent! Or share something else God is doing or has done in your life. I recently sent a hand-written letter of apology to my eldest grandson with excellent results. Just make contact any way you can! I can't encourage you enough to get started ASAP!

One word of warning before you continue: the key component to your grandparenting connection with your Gkids is your kids! Yes, your kids. They are the conduit through which you interact with your Gkids. As I do, you also may know of some grandparents who are not able to interact with their Gkids at all because their Gkids' parents won't allow it.

I trust that nothing within the pages of this book will hinder your relationship with your Gkids' parents – your kids! The goal is for us to partner with our children in the lives of our Gkids. To be part of a team with them, not their opponent. To support them and not to barge in and do it 'our way.' To be their ally and not to be a threat to their parenting. We want them to extend their trust to us, and then to feel free to contact us when help is needed. The parent is the key, so we should not damage that relationship and jeopardize our ministry to our Gkids!

ACTION PLAN – CHAPTER FIVE

What difference do you anticipate being intentional will mean to you as a grandparent?

What method of communication do you plan to use with your Gkids and when do you plan to start?

CHAPTER SIX

Impacting Our Family Tree For Generations

Before starting this chapter, let's look at two fellows named Charles. One is Charlie Brown of Peanuts fame and the other is Charles Spurgeon of preaching fame. Charlie Brown liked to play the child endangering game of Jarts, also called Lawn Darts! Whoever thought of giving kids big, sharp objects and telling them to throw them around??? To play Jarts you were supposed to put a circular ring on the ground, and then throw your jarts towards the ring hoping to stick your jart inside the ring. Charlie found his own way to succeed. He would first throw his jart, then he would take the ring to where his jart had landed and put the ring around his jart! That way he hit it every time. Maybe some of you grandparent that same way!

Charles Spurgeon had a different plan than Charlie Brown. He gave us a target to aim for as he said this, "A good character is the best tombstone. Those who loved you and were helped by you (your Gkids) will remember you when forget-me-nots have withered. Carve your name on hearts, not on marble." This is also my goal for you, and I'll repeat it often: for you to intentionally, purposefully, wisely and proactively carve your spiritual legacy on the hearts of each of your grand-children!

Your impact on thousands! Here are some thoughts regarding your potential generational impact as a Godly grandparent. Yes, you read that word thousands correctly. In the Ten Commandments, God states that He shows mercy unto thousands. Could that be part of your impact on your family tree starting with you? Yes!

First, impacting thousands! You'll have to trust me regarding the following math. If just ONE of your Gkids continues your spiritual legacy, in 10 generations or approximately 300 years, 1,000 people directly related to you will be touched by YOUR life. In 20 generations, or app. 600 years, that number jumps to a whopping one million!

You might say that we're in the end times so this number of years won't transpire. But it may, as people were probably saying this same thing during the Black Plague. I'm sure they didn't think the world was going to continue very long, but it has! The above assumes that each child in a generation is married and has four kids. That may seem to be a large family, but remember that just a few generations back, families of 6 – 9 kids were common.

In addition, let's assume you follow through with some of the information in this book and make a positive Godly impact on your Gkids. And let's assume that being a Christ-follower is strong in you, your kids, your Gkids, and your great Gkids. However, things go south spiritually for your great, great Gkids. Where are you at this time? In heaven watching. Yet in Psalm 22:31a we are told, *"You will proclaim His righteousness, declaring to a people yet unborn!"* So even though you are no longer living on earth, your impact can still be made on those currently not yet alive! And because YOU impressed the life of your Gkids, they do the SAME to their Gkids (your great, great

Gkids who no longer are close to Jesus). And that impact changes the course of your great, great Gkids' lives and returns your entire family tree back to Jesus! What joy will be yours in heaven as you watch the impressions you made on your Gkids' lives be imparted to your great, great Gkids! I tear up when I consider that potential!

Your potential impact as a Godly grandparent is truly amazing. Lord, may it be so!

Be THE grandparent! Throughout the book, I'll be sharing a few stories from my own family and this one is a positive one. By sharing actual stories, the intent is not to hurt anyone, but to emphasize a point based on actual experience. My sister had boys, and she told them they were going to see their Grandma. The boys were excited, but when they drove into the driveway, the kids shouted, "Oh no, not that Grandma!" They thought they were going to see my Mom!

Endeavor not to be *that* grandparent, but to be *the* grandparent your Gkids want to see. Much more will be written on this as we begin to give you various tools to add to your Godly grandparenting toolbox!

ACTION PLAN – CHAPTER SIX

How does being a Godly grandparent who impacts your family tree for generations change your attitude and behavior towards your grandparenting?

CHAPTER SEVEN

Time and Wisdom

I remember a friend sharing a time when he was with his Gkids at a multi-level store with an escalator. They wanted to go up and down that device over and over again. He recalled that as a parent he was too busy – you know, things to do; places to go; people to see. But as a grandparent, he was able to go up and down as many times as they wanted. As grandparents, we have a chance to slow down a bit; to be as one person said – the only ones who have time to listen. Plus, we also have the wisdom to make wise choices regarding our Gkids.

Regarding time, this *getting old* thing frustrated me as I neared 60. I became discouraged. Normally an upbeat person with no time to be depressed, this number was getting to me. I viewed it as a definite time of physical deterioration, knowing my physical abilities would continue to go downhill until the end. Sure, I could do plan B activities, which would be less demanding on my body, but if I had wanted to do them previously, I would have. Now, I was going to be forced to make some changes. And I didn't like it one bit.

But God intervened! Somehow, I still don't know how, I began to realize that God's plan regarding aging was the best plan. Just writing that sounds foolish, as I don't think Almighty God was waiting around for that confirmation from little me! Yes, getting old is at least partially bad news, but my perspective soon changed. By getting old, the physical activity aspect of my life was going to be minimized or changed, but this would result in more time available to do others things – things that were far more important than sports!

Along with the extra time, the stuff I'd been through had given me some wisdom, and my age meant I knew more people than ever to share that wisdom with. The light went on! With the gift of time and the blessing of wisdom, I could transition into relationships rather than activities. Let me repeat that – a time to transition into relationships rather than activities.

Yes, the day I would die would be the worst physical day of my life, but that very same day could be the very BEST relational day of my life. I saw this gift of time and the blessing of wisdom as God's plan for us, especially as grandparents! Plus, God considers our relationships as far more valuable than whatever physical activity we might enjoy. My depression lifted; my purpose was renewed!

As grandparents, many of us now have extra time, so the question becomes 'what are we going to do with it.' I know some of you are thinking 'now that I'm retired, I'm busier than ever.' Hopefully your not wasting your days on superficial activities, as possibly the most important thing you could be doing is spending time with your Gkids! Sounds obvious, but I talked with a friend who shared about her busy life and her Gkids. Suddenly she stopped herself in midsentence and then said, "I'm making the same mistake I made with my kids." She realized she wasn't spending enough time with her Gkids. Sometime later I talked with her husband who told me she had retired and was spending much more time with her Gkids!

This time thing is REALLY important! By far the most common response to 'why was your grandparent special' was that their grandparent proactively spent time with them participating in the things the Gkids wanted to do. A big key to successful grandparenting – spend time with your Gkids and use that time wisely and sacrificially! The extra time on the escalator was a good use of time, but God tells us an even better way. A way that impresses their hearts! Deuteronomy 6:6-10 teaches, *"These words I am commanding you today are to be upon your hearts. And you shall* **teach them** *diligently to your children and* **speak of them** *when you* **sit** *at home and when you* **walk** *along the road, when you* **lie down** *and when you* **get up.** **Tie them** *as reminders on your hands and* **bind them** *on your foreheads.* **Write them** *on the doorposts of your houses and on your gates."*

Wow! That's like all the time and everywhere! You get the point! Most of us, including me, fall far short of this standard. But we can improve! An easy way is to do two things. First, ask yourself this question, 'What message am I sending to my Gkids if they were to evaluate my schedule?' What would they consider to be the most important aspect of your life as indicated by what you choose to do? As you consider this, consider ways to alter your schedule to reflect the importance of leaving a Godly legacy in the life of each of your Gkids.

One person told me how her Grandpa came one Saturday a month and was there to wake her up that morning. It wasn't until far later that she realized what it took for him to do this. He was impacting her life, but at a cost. He lived four hours away and had to get up at 3 in the morning to make the drive to be there in time to wake her up. At the time, it didn't make much of an impression. Later, and for the rest of her life, it did! Remember, actions speak louder than words! Much louder.

Also, what is your house saying? We don't tie things on our hands; bind things on our foreheads; or write on our doors and gates. But we do have various things on our walls within our home.

Do they tell visitors AND our Gkids that this is a home in which God is the top priority? When our Gkids come over, our home does speak! What are your walls saying? Driving through North Carolina, I repeatedly saw 'Thank You Jesus' signs on various yards. My plan is to put one of those in my front yard!

ACTION PLAN – CHAPTER SEVEN

How effective has your use of time been with your Gkids? What changes can you make?

What changes can you make in your home to declare it is a Godly place?

What are practical ways you can strengthen family relationships while your body weakens?

CHAPTER EIGHT

The Blessing of Wisdom

What about this blessing of wisdom? One way to define it might be living a life characterized by the Fruit of the Spirit. We're talking about God's wisdom, not the secular version. Not knowledge, but applied knowledge! As grandparents, we have gone through lots of experiences and sometimes don't realize how much wisdom God has imparted to us during our journey. We must not waste it – it must be shared with our Gkids in a way that they will receive it! In Proverbs 15:2 we read, *The tongue of the wise makes knowledge acceptable, but the mouth of fools spouts folly.* When we share God's wisdom, we don't want to be spouting folly, but we should share words that they listen to. They might not initially believe what we say, but we will at least be heard.

When our precious Gkids are small, we may not be imparting much wisdom. But we can use this time to lay a strong foundation of relationship so that later they will be confident in our love for them and will talk with us about important things. Because they are willing to listen to us, one of the things we must share is a Biblical worldview. Public schools and non-Christian friends certainly will share competing worldviews, so we must be prepared to have a wise tongue when the opportunity to share our beliefs presents itself. Reading Proverbs regularly and asking for wisdom WILL increase your Godly wisdom!

Here are two analogies which might help you connect with your Gkids. I use analogies partly because Jesus did, as He taught along the way utilizing the common to enlighten His followers about God's ways. These analogies are designed to assist in your communication with questioning Gkids, and hopefully will lend credibility to your beliefs, rather than just saying, 'The Bible says it, so you should believe it!'

The first is comparing the Bible to a car owner's manual. When one buys a new car, the manufacturer equips each car with instructions as to how to most effectively utilize and maintain that car. And NO one objects. They know better than applying a motorcycle owner's manual to the maintenance of a car. The new owners actually want the creator of their car to tell them the best way to deal with their specific model. However, when it comes to the Bible and God advising His created beings to follow His guidelines for their best life, we object. But if we welcome an owner's manual for a car, we should much more desire a manual for living. When your Gkids accept the idea of a car owner's manual, then they just might accept God's word in a similar fashion.

The second is utilizing sports when your Gkids question all the 'rules' in the Bible. I'll pick baseball. You could ask them what it would be like to play baseball without rules. You could swing and miss and say you hit a home run! Or you could catch a ground ball and say the batter is out. Or you could pitch one to the backstop and call it a strike. You get the idea. Baseball, or any game, could not be played at all without rules. And the game of life cannot either. No rules = anarchy and chaos. God's rules are designed for us to be able to have the potential to live in harmony and peace. Baseball needs rules, so does life. And who better to make the rules for baseball than the ones who began the game. Same with our Creator! I trust these and other analogies will give you a wise tongue when you share your knowledge about God and the Bible.

ACTION PLAN – CHAPTER EIGHT

Which analogy, owner's manual or sports, do you see yourself using with your Gkids? How?

Have you minimized your personal wisdom in the past? If so, how can you increase your confidence, and make sure you have a wise tongue in the future?

CHAPTER NINE

Words – Helpful Or Hurtful

One thing we humans do a lot of is talk! Words are everywhere like a tsunami flowing into our ears and out of our mouths. Since we talk so much, it is important to examine our words and see where we stand! First a quick quiz, and I'm predicting you'll get an A on the first one, and most will score an F on the second one. Here you go – Silence is _____! Yep, you know this secular one – Silence is golden! Now a Biblical quiz – In Ephesians 4:29 it reads, *'your words are to give _____ to the hearer.'* This is a tougher one – take a minute and don't just guess! Drum roll please, and the answer is - to give GRACE to the hearer! The world has done a good job of getting us to know the silence is golden phrase, yet we should know the Biblical one just as well or even better.

If grace is giving something to someone they don't deserve, when our words give grace to the hearer, our words of grace might not match what the action warranted – but that's God's way! One of the young people I interviewed shared that her Grandma thought she was speaking words which were helpful, but actually her words were hurtful. Like most teens, she was body sensitive and was well aware of her body's shortcomings. Grandma's seemingly constructive comments about some of her physical traits ended up hurting her.

While giving a workshop, an elderly Grandma was crying the session after I spoke about our words. When I asked her why, her response was that she had felt that as a Grandma, she now had the platform to pretty much say whatever she wanted. When she considered all she had said over the years, she knew many of those words were hurtful and that brought out the tears. I encouraged her to seek forgiveness and as Philippians says, *'to reach forward to what lies ahead!'* I'm confident she did just that!

So, what words did you enjoy hearing when you were growing up? My Mom would regularly kind of poke my daughter and say, "Looks like you've gained a little weight." Although not a direct cause and effect, my not overweight adult daughter has struggled with her weight all of her life. How about words like 'I see you're starting to get pimples' or 'Do you spend every waking hour on your cell phone' – These types of comments should be in the silence is golden category, but far too often they escape our lips.

As Godly grandparents, if our words to our Gkids are not words of grace, we shouldn't be saying them. Does that mean we never try to help with our words? No, but being helpful, not hurtful, is the key. And positive words of encouragement can always be found. That doesn't mean saying 'I see you're losing weight' or 'Looks like those pimples are going away.' But it does mean that you know their strengths and the things they do well, and then using words that address those should always fall in the helpful category.

Also in Ephesians 4, this time in verse 15, we are told to speak the truth in love. I remember hearing Chuck Swindoll giving an illustration of doing just that in a difficult situation. Many people would show him their babies expecting a positive comment. However, he shared that some of them were not the best looking of babies, so what to do. Well, to follow God's directive to speak the truth in love, he would loudly and enthusiastically state, "Now that's a baby!" Truth spoken in love.

Our words must reflect the wisdom God has given us, and they cannot be words that 'major in the minors.' We'll explore this in depth later, but for now we must avoid having our Gkids turn us off because they have heard us comment about every little thing all of the time. One workshop attendee shared that before he met Jesus, that is what he did – nitpicked about the minors. He now is trying to share Jesus with them, something major, but his kids have basically shut down and he senses them doing the La la la la la thing when he talks.

My suggestion to you when talking to your Gkids is that you have two choices: silence or words of grace! Who wouldn't want to share almost anything if they knew they were not going to be judged, but they were going to get a response of grace or merely no commentary about it at all. This is a major part of being 'the' grandparent that your Gkids go to during challenging times in their lives. Because your words have consistently been words of grace or no words at all, you might be the only person in their lives whom your Gkids can come to with confidence as to the response they'll receive! I've worked with teens much of my life, and I KNOW challenging times regularly invade their lives. They need someone to talk to, and when you're careful with your words, that person will be you!

Unintentional Impressions. When talking with my own kids about our parenting, we came to realize there were impressions our words had made on them that were nowhere near our intent. We thought we weren't demanding parents in regards to grades, and that we merely communicated that grades were important. When our son said we wanted all 'A's' on his report card, we responded with, "No way, we just wanted you to do your best." He then gave us an example of one time his report card had five 'A's and one 'B.' Our response was "What's up with the B?" Our intent was just to find out why this class had been more of a challenge for him. His take on our comment was MUCH different – His take was that we only were satisfied if he brought home all 'A's.

Sadly, what we communicate can be the exact opposite of our intent, and what's caught is often so much more important than what's taught. To help clarify, I'll refer to an 'inner package' and an 'outer package.' I think we would all agree that the Lord is more concerned with our inner package – attitude, character, spirituality, the Fruit of the Spirit, and more. As I Samuel 16:7a tells us, *"People judge by the outward appearance, but God looks upon the heart!"* So it follows that we also should be primarily concerned about our Gkids' inner package, not their outer package – looks, grades, abilities, athleticism, clothes, etc.

BUT DO WE?

As we focus on the wise use of our words, let's explore one area of verbal communication – questions! Why questions? When we ask about something, we express interest. You might be talking with someone and interject a question about a specific thing they were talking about. That question expresses interest! When I had a speaker talk to my high school classes, I had a little trick to make them think they were the most interesting speaker ever. The students were required to write a one-page paper in response to the presentation, OR ask two questions! Guess which one most of them picked! When the speaker stopped and said, "Are there any questions," hands shot up all over the room. A look of 'Wow, I'm good!' immediately appeared on the speakers' faces!

Let's restrict it even further to questions we might ask our Gkids. As you read the following, consider it within the backdrop of impressing their inner or outer package. Let's assume some of your

Gkids are staying with you for a week during the school year. What are some of the questions you might ask them during this week and what message are you sending? Is it possible that your intentions won't match the impressions you're actually making on their hearts and minds?

Here are some typical questions most of us would probably ask: How did you do in school today? Have you done your homework? Did you clean up your mess and brush your teeth? Do you have any tests or projects coming up? How are your grades doing? How are you doing on your team? Do you have a boyfriend or girlfriend yet?

Are any of these questions inherently bad – NO! But evaluated against the inner and outer package criteria, what was the focus of each question? That's right – the outer package. But weren't we supposed to be more concerned about their inner package? Hence the problem!

How about questions which focus on their inner package and move them towards being like Jesus? These inner package questions are a bit harder to come up with, but let's try: Are you doing any type of daily devotions? Do you have any friends who might want to go to youth group/Awanas – I'll pick them up? Is there anything going on in your life that I could pray for? Did you see God at work today during school? In what ways were you a good teammate at practice today? Have you committed your season/performance to God?

At first glance, this might seem a bit extreme. But by asking this type of question, the impression we make on our Gkids is that we PRIORITIZE their inner package! Should we keep the outer package questions? Sure! But they must not be all we ask, nor should they dominate our questioning. To impress their hearts with what God is concerned about, we must ask inner package questions! It just might be that young people leave the church because their life focus becomes their outer package, as a direct result of the continual outer package questions thrown their way. After a continual barrage of those questions, they might conclude, 'after all, what you were constantly concerned about is exactly what the focus of my life is now.' The outer package!

As a parent, I was unintentionally guilty of this, and don't want to rewrite those outer package questions on the hearts and minds of my Gkids! How about you?

This will not be an easy transition. My wife and I failed at it with our son when he was experiencing job difficulties. We questioned how the job was going, would his finances be OK, were there any other job options and such. Yes, these were good and relevant questions, but the focus of our questions should have been his INNER package. Was he at peace, was his character growing through this process, how was his trust and dependence on God doing?

Thankfully, we caught ourselves and moved away from the outer package questions to the inner package ones. And surprise, surprise – his anxiety lessened, his outlook changed, and he was more at peace! Hopefully, we've learned our lesson!

ACTION PLAN – CHAPTER NINE

Did you answer correctly the question on our words extending grace? Cite an example of how this could have changed a previous interaction with one of your Gkids.

Are you aware of any unintentional impression you have made on your kids or Gkids? How could you have spoken differently?

List some inner package questions you WILL use with your Gkids.

CHAPTER TEN

Becoming A Memory Maker

Various movies have been made about God's gift of memory. Stories of losing one's memory or not having a memory at all litter the big screen. We can't imagine living without memories, yet there are some events in all of our lives which we might want to quickly erase if we had that power. However, we can't. The good and the bad memories stay with us. Today, you could start writing and fill a book of your personal memories; some in vivid detail. One of the problems with our memory; however, is that even though we can remember specific details about childhood experiences, yet we can't remember what our spouse said five minutes ago!

Although memories are extremely important, we don't often consider intentionally making memories in the minds of others. Well, as grandparents, being an intentional memory maker is something we should definitely be doing.

So what's the big deal about being a memory maker? Let's do the math in regards to the impact we have with our Gkids. Using the average age that people become grandparents in the U.S. as

50, and the average life expectancy of 78, we will physically grandparent our eldest grandchild 28 years. Even less for the rest of the crew.

Now the math! That means that we will physically interact for 36% of both of our lives. Since it is even less for the rest of our Gkids, I'll use the fraction 1/3 as a general figure. If 1/3 of our lives will be together, we will spend a whopping 2/3 of our Gkids' lives ONLY IN THEIR MEMORY! When we also factor in that we aren't with them physically 24/7 during the first 1/3 of their lives, it becomes obvious where we primarily involve ourselves with them – within their memories!

I know this end-of-life kind of talk could sound a bit morbid, but it is necessary. The math doesn't lie. As grandparents, we are primarily 'Memory Makers!' So, what are we going to do about it?

First, if we're going to intentionally make memories, we have to know how memories are made! Within our brain, this process is extremely complex and not totally understood. Many factors can be involved, but I'll focus on only two things which help us create memories in our Gkids. These two are 'the unique' and 'the repetitive.'

Create! Yes, we are to intentionally and purposefully create memories within the minds of our Gkids. Remember the ceramic pieces? Not just any memories, but ones which make an impression on their hearts leading them to love God, which is the number one commandment from Jesus. Creating memories is a grand opportunity for grandparents!

So how can we use 'the unique' to make memories? Simple, do unique things with your Gkids, which no one else will be doing! And if these activities are not only unique, but also special, they have a far better chance of being remembered. And not special to you, but special to them! We have to go back to school, meaning we are to make the effort to LEARN as much about each of our Gkids as we can, so our actions and words will be meaningful to them individually.

All of these unique and special times must fall within the approval of the parents! It may take a bit of persuading, but the conduit to our Gkids, their parents, must at least be OK with what we're doing! Now, anything we try will be a win/win. Whether the times together are good or bad, they will be stuck in their memory as long as they live. Even bad memories turn into funny stories after a time! Remember, we'll be gone and only our memories will remain.

Consider your grandparents for a moment. What memories have they left you with? Are they the memories you want to implant in your Gkids' minds, or will you need to take a different route? I only remember my grandparents being very nice people. As a family, we saw each one every other Sunday, but that was it. We didn't have any one-on-one time, and they never attended any of my games or events. They were just nice people. I want to be that as well, but so much more!

As we create memories with our Gkids, their spiritual impact cannot be minimized. Our Gkids' minds should be filled with memories of us, and MANY of those memories should have a spiritual overtone or influence. By knowing each of your Gkids, that will allow you to have your own individual memory making plan, and I'll throw some generic 'memory makers' your way.

One suggestion would be celebrating their spiritual birthday. Most of us are already involved in their physical birthday, but as Godly grandparents, the spiritual or inner package should be even more important! Try to find out when they asked Jesus to be their Savior. Mark it on your calendar. Circle it! And then do something for each of those birthdays with the same enthusiasm or more than the date of their actual birth. The information in the Appendix expands on this concept.

If you are able to celebrate their spiritual birthday, it ends up being both unique and repetitive, resulting in a definite memory. And when we're gone, that date will either encourage them or haunt them depending on their relationship with Jesus – another win/win! Don't feel the pressure of doing something elaborate on that day, but DO something.

I know of a family that buried a memory box. They had their Gkids bring some items of clothing and other 'stuff' which they recently valued, and they would put them in a sealed container and literally bury the box! Five years later, they would gather the Gkids and dig up the buried treasure. Clothes that no longer fit or were out of style brought much laughter to the event, plus some 'I remember that doll/thing' would cement that day into their memory. And a written note from you about them, including how they were doing spiritually, could be added to the memory box!

Cousins' camp is also a memory maker. This is a time where you bring as many of the Gkids as you can together for as long as you can handle it! Their ages determine the type of activities, but make it a camp-like atmosphere with crafts, games, spiritual time, sleeping over – as fun as you can for as long as you can. Start small, do your best, create memories! It's not easy and may not be perfect, but it definitely brings the Gkids together and creates collective memories they will later share as cousins.

Firsts also become unique and special. The 'first' time they ever fished, rode a horse, went to church camp, snapped their fingers, etc. These firsts will always be a memory of Grandma and Grandpa. I took my eldest grandson to his first major college football game. Sadly, it was over 100 degrees and we left at halftime, but a memory was made. And if the 'first' becomes something they do for a hobby or even career, your influence in that area will never be forgotten!

What about repetition? Consistency over time is something that should characterize our lives as Godly grandparents, and this consistency will create memories! This memory-making tool can often be used by way of our speech. My wife and I have a goal that our Gkids are aware of what an awesome creator God is. We then speak of that often when out and about with them. Recently, that memory was rewarded when one of our Gkids' parents shared how they were out in God's creation and their son kept remarking about how awesome God was to create all the stuff they were seeing!

I know of a Grandma who was given the nickname of Scripture Judy (not her real name). This was because when she was with her Gkids, she always had a written verse or more to share with them. Then she gave a written copy of the verses to them. She has passed away, but Scripture Judy is firmly implanted in the memory of each of her Gkids.

When you're gone and your Gkids are together talking about you – maybe at your funeral – what will they be saying about you with the word always in it? 'Papa always used to ????' 'When Grandma saw us she would always ????' Consistency, repetition, intentionality, purpose – like it or not, you ARE a Memory Maker. The type of memories you make depends on you!

ACTION PLAN – CHAPTER TEN

Did the percentage of time you actually physically spend with your Gkids surprise you? List ways you can spend more time with them.

Write some of the memories you have about your grandparents. Then write what memories you desire to create in your Gkids' lives.

CHAPTER ELEVEN

Three Intriguing Thoughts

This chapter will present three short thoughts intended to stimulate your thinking and make you a better Godly grandparent. In writing this book, I'm aware that not everything will fit your grandparenting style. But the intention is for you to consider the many avenues you could take, and then for you to decide which to implement.

Pre-planning. When interacting with our kids and Gkids, we definitely need to do some advanced planning to save us from words or actions we won't be able to retrieve. Things don't always turn out the right way – meaning the way we want them to – so we need to plan for curve balls!

What one couple who attended a workshop did illustrates this point perfectly. They were excited about their first Gkid's Christmas with them. Knowing they weren't going to have many more Gkids, they knew this first Christmas was going to be very special for them and were really looking forward to it. However, they chose to pre-plan for the unexpected. They were well aware of how busy their son and daughter-in-law were, as she was interning as a doctor and he was working on his doctorate.

The chances of their kids being too busy for any type of family Christmas lurked dangerously ahead. Proactively and intentionally, they decided that if this first Gkid's Christmas failed to materialize, they would be gracious and understanding about it. Sure enough, they got the call that Christmas was not going to happen. The grandparents adhered to their plan and responded in an understanding manner, while hiding their hurt feelings. Although saddened, they didn't lash out in frustration because of their pre-planning.

But that's not the end of the story. After Christmas, the daughter-in-law called and apologized for missing Christmas. Then she promised them that it would NEVER happen again, and they would always spend time with them at Christmas! There were no long-lasting hurts from words angrily spoken and the future looked great! Definitely a reason to pre-plan.

Pre-framing. This concept is similar to pre-planning, but different in that in pre-framing, we are wise enough to KNOW what surely will happen in various scenarios. The following directly illustrates the importance of pre-framing. A couple shared what they did with the parents of their Gkids – their kids! Babysitting was in their very near future, so they pre-framed what they KNEW was going to happen.

They were experienced enough to predict issues arising when babysitting: types of food, discipline, bedtime, etc. After pre-framing the various challenges, they asked their kids what, as parents, they desired when the grandparents were babysitting. A good discussion ensued, agreement was reached, and things went well. BUT an unexpected blessing also resulted. Their kids now had confidence in their parents in terms of coming to them for advice about raising their kids. Something the grandparents never thought would happen. They became a team in the raising of the Gkids. A specific result from wise pre-framing!

The Holy Spirit. I checked with a few pastors before putting this in my workshop, and they couldn't say it was directly in the Bible, but they felt it did not contradict any Biblical teaching. The concept is in reference to how the Trinity is exemplified by humans.

I believe parents reflect to kids the role of Father God. They hold a position of authority and have the responsibility to teach and guide. Jesus is represented in the lives of those who have a spiritual impact on us. We see Jesus in those lives. Examples would be youth pastors and Christ-following adults or peers.

Then who displays the attributes of the Holy Spirit? I believe the answer is grandparents! For one, we hold the position of one who comforts. Our consistency brings a certainty to our Gkids, and that certainty gives them comfort. We can be their paraclete – one who walks beside them, advocates for them, and helps them. We also can assist them in recognizing their sin and their need for Jesus in a way no one else could. All of these are aspects of what the Holy Spirit does in our lives, and we can extend those qualities to our Gkids. What a privilege and WHAT a responsibility! And with God's help, we can do it!

ACTION PLAN – CHAPTER ELEVEN

Write a specific example of how you can utilize both Pre-Planning and Pre-Framing with your kids and/or Gkids.

Does the concept of grandparents serving as Holy Spirit ring true with you? How can you bring comfort to your Gkids?

CHAPTER TWELVE

Leaving A Legacy

Like it or not, we will all leave a legacy. It's not a choice, it's a given. The question is: What type of legacy will we leave to our Gkids? Remember Proverbs 13:22 – *A good grandparent leaves an inheritance* (or legacy) *to their grandchildren.*

I'll start by quoting what someone wrote regarding their two sets of grandparents using initials for privacy. As you read, consider what type of legacy was imprinted on this grandchild by the respective set of grandparents. I also highlighted in bold the impression they made on her heart – our number one priority!

> "I always **felt** loved and accepted by M and P. Not that G and G don't love me, but there have been times in my life where I have **felt** very judged by them because some decisions I've made (or didn't make) didn't match up with what they thought/expected I should do. Grandparents need to remember that things have changed from when they were our age and just because they did something one way doesn't mean we are "bad" if we don't do things the same way! M and P NEVER made me **feel** like I was a total screw-up (even

when I was) . . . they gently and lovingly let me know when they thought I was on the wrong path and also let me know that they would do WHATEVER it took to help me turn things around; that their love was unconditional. Honestly, there have been times in my life where I've **felt** like receiving love from G and G was conditional on whether or not they approved of where I was at in my life, and that strained our relationship. . . a lot. I've always had a much more open relationship with M and P than with G and G, for this reason alone. I knew I could talk to M and P about anything without **feeling** like they didn't love me anymore, whereas, if I were to talk to G/G about the same things, I would **feel** like they loved me less because of their harsh reactions or words."

Yes, our legacy will impact our grandkids either for good, for bad, or it may just be neutral. Our goal needs to be leaving a legacy like M and P above, not G and G. And being intentional and proactive WILL make that happen.

As we talk with our Gkids about life and our Biblical worldview, a Proverbs 15:2 reminder should guide us, *"The tongue of the wise makes knowledge acceptable."* Our knowledge may be true, but if we can't share it in a way that they will at least listen to us and find us credible, we've lost before we've started.

One of the younger generation's favorite words is 'whatever.' Not my personal favorite that's for sure! Moral absolutes are the compass of truth, but they are currently being attacked at every level. In early Biblical days, 'everyone did that which was right in their own eyes.' In the 60's, 'do your own thing' became the mantra. Plus, the number one tenet of Satanism is 'do what thou wilt.' A popular singing duo has 'Do what thou wilt' as part of their clothing line, so it's not some faraway concept to our Gkids. All of these are in direct opposition to a Biblical worldview and have infiltrated our culture in far too many ways. Although we need to share that there is absolute truth, we better have 'the tongue of the wise.'

Remember the 'owner's manual' and 'sports' analogies? These can help make our knowledge acceptable and impact the quality of our spiritual legacy! One other illustration may help. We run into trouble when we view the Bible through the lens of life's circumstances. This means we evaluate the Bible in light of wars, famines, and other catastrophic events. However, looking at life through the lens of the Bible is what we should encourage our Gkids to do.

The question is not how do the events in life adjust our view of the Bible, but how does the Bible impact our response to difficult aspects of life. When we encourage our Gkids to think this way, they can question everything, as the Bible will lead them to truth and faith! A great legacy!

Much of our legacy will be a result of what we've modeled to our Gkids. The old adage that actions speak louder than words definitely applies here. How are you doing in this area? I became aware of a Mom who told her 4-year-old to say they were 3 so they could get in an amusement park at a lesser price. That worked until she was pulled over for speeding, and her 4-year-old was in an age-appropriate car seat. However, when the officer came to the car and the Mom stated that the child seat was OK because she was 4, her child shouted out, "No Mom, I'm 3, remember!"

Here are some tough modeling questions: Do you take your Gkids somewhere and say they're a different age so that the admission is cheaper? Is your integrity only worth saving $20 at Disneyland? Do you demonstrate you value truth above all, or do you give them the impression that 'white' lies are OK? Do you model that you trust God first when difficulties arise, or do you do everything else and then finally pray over it? How do you respond to bad news – having confidence in our Creator and being confident in Romans 8:28, or is worrying your usual response? Is God your number one concern or only a Sunday thing? The answers to these questions give you some idea of how your legacy is unfolding.

Be an inspiration! Your legacy will point them somewhere, hopefully in God's direction, but we should even go further. We also are to inspire them, which is much harder but important! If a bad legacy of broken relationships is currently 'written' in your family, what is that communicating to your Gkids? If they see that this is OK with you, then you will be modeling something you would never want them to do in their relationship with you. Actions do speak louder than words. Therefore, we should make every effort to intentionally rebuild any negative relationship.

Someone I know had a terrible relationship with her Mother-in-law. When grandkids came, their relationship improved greatly, but no real healing had occurred and there still is a shadow over their family relationships. We are to admit any guilt (everybody has some role in the start or ongoing dysfunction), swallow our pride, and ask for forgiveness! God is a God of reconciliation, so we are to follow His example in attempting to restore the legacy of broken relationships with our family members.

As grandparents, we can be compared to the pace car at a NASCAR race. After an incident on the track, the pace car leads the racers around the track and no one can go faster than it. We can set the pace in our families, and we surely should set the pace when it comes to reconciliation. YOU can be the pacesetter for your family in terms of restoration or attempts to do so! If others have hurt or offended you, remember the lengths God went to in an effort to restore your relationship with Him – Jesus' sacrifice. We too may need to 'suffer' or sacrifice a bit to restore a difficult one! Even if it is impossible, our efforts will demonstrate to our Gkids that we are doing everything in our power to reconcile – an important legacy to leave with them!

Remember Deuteronomy 4:9,10 where God tells us to *'make known'* to our Gkids the things He has done in our lives?' One way to accomplish this is to write these down in some format starting with the first time God's hand touched your life until now. Mine started at conception! It wasn't a miraculous conception, but it surely shouldn't have happened; yet here I am! My second one was my birth. Because of a variety of circumstances, it looked like I wasn't going to make it; yet here I am! Yours may not start as early in life as mine, but write down the legacy of what God has done in your life! This also could be a video and could even be given to them after you're gone.

Our legacy will be all-encompassing, and one way to leave a lasting legacy or memory is to create things that last. Making cookies is a fun activity and should be a must as we interact with our Gkids. But creating something that lasts makes a generational connection far after the cookies are gone. An example would be to create a detailed family history. It may not be appreciated when the Gkids are young, but someday they will as it can forge a forever connection! I once saw a bumper sticker stating 'we're spending our children's inheritance.' Let's not live like our bumper sticker should be – I'm squandering my Gkids' legacy!

Other legacies include having integrity, honoring parents, being honest, sharing that life is eternal as we are spiritual beings trapped in earth suits, sharing accounts of God's faithfulness, prioritizing people not money or things, having the ability to endure suffering/hardship and more. We give them footprints to follow. Remember, your example speaks loudly!

If you want to leave a legacy that will never die, be the grandparent your Gkids want to be around. A girl I talked with is seeing her grandparent with Alzheimer's, but she isn't visiting the one who is healthy because of the legacy that grandparent left with her.

Many of us know of Mr. Rogers. What you might not know is this: the foundation for Mr. Rogers' TV show was inspired by his special relationship with his grandfather! When Mr. Rogers visited his grandfather, he remembers him saying that his grandson should always be himself. His words made Mr. Rogers feel special. As a result, he made it his ministry to make others be able to share that same special feeling. Thanks Grandpa!!!

Finally, where do people speak of people's past? Funerals. I remember my son being responsible for the eulogy at my Dad's funeral. He spoke about a specific characteristic of his Grandpa, which I didn't know had impacted his life. At your funeral, what attributes would your Gkids share about you? The life you led will be the life they share! To emphasize this, as part of this chapter's action plan, you will write a short 'legacy statement' as if it were being written by your Gkids. Choose a Godly legacy!

ACTION PLAN – CHAPTER TWELVE

Write your epitaph as it might appear on a large tombstone. Write it as though your Gkids were writing it. List as many adjectives as you deem appropriate.

You are in some control as to what is written above when it really happens. List some specific things you need to be doing now to make the above a reality.

Is there a current family relationship in need of reconciliation? If so, how can you be proactive in that process?

CHAPTER THIRTEEN

Leaving and Bestowing a Blessing

Before we explore this topic, let me share a quote from Dietrich Bonhoeffer – "If human beings (grandparents) have passed on to loved ones (Gkids) and to many the blessing they have themselves received, then they have surely fulfilled the most important thing in life; then they have surely themselves become persons happy in God and have made others (Gkids) happy in God."

Blessing! Let me first ask you a couple of questions about the word blessing. Did you have an adult speak a blessing into your life? Would you be comfortable demonstrating a spoken blessing to others or is it more like trying to speak Greek? After this chapter, I am convinced you will be confidently speaking blessings to your Gkids and others! Gary Smalley and John Trent wrote, *The Blessing*. God intended giving blessings as a responsibility of families, and as grandparents, we are in a perfect spot to give blessings to our Gkids! Our legacy is the life we live, but a blessing is what we give – primarily words and touch. Unlike our legacy, which happens regardless, giving a blessing is a choice – choose wisely!

Blessing is done in two ways: being a blessing and/or bestowing one. First, to be a blessing is to be accepting. At some point that may be all your Gkids need. By being non-judgmental and silent about some of their choices, you will be a blessing. By being a consistent encourager, you will be a blessing. When you fight for them or don't make them feel like less of a person, you will be a blessing. And in general, you will always be a blessing to your Gkids when you are sincere and genuine. When you are sincerely interested in what they are interested in and genuinely excited for them, they will consider themselves blessed!

Another person I talked with shared how her Grandma was the opposite of being sincere and genuine. The girl played volleyball and her Grandma hadn't come to any of her games. She was excited when her Grandma said she would come to one, especially since it was a long way away. She assumed Grandma was sincerely interested, but she wasn't, nor was she genuinely excited. Between points, the girl would sneak a look up to Grandma in the bleachers. There she saw her messing with her fingernails and not paying any attention to her. No, we are to be sincerely interested and genuinely excited for them – even if we're not big fans of the event they are participating in!!!

Bestowing a blessing. After reading the next few pages, I trust you will find speaking a blessing to your grandchildren to be a simple and rewarding task! Even if your blessing is not done well, the impact of this blessing is like an American Olympic diver compared to a Chinese diver. The American diver may not be as pretty as their opponents, but they do make a bigger splash in the water! Don't worry if your blessing isn't pretty, because it's more important for it to have a big impact – a big splash! Speaking blessings will have a dynamic impact for generations!

So, what is the impact of speaking a blessing into the lives of your Gkids? Glad you asked! For one, you will immediately be set apart in their lives! I've asked many grandparents if they had people speaking a blessing into their lives and very few had, much less from a grandparent. So you will be different! You will be uniquely special, as your Gkids may not be receiving a spoken blessing from anyone else but YOU!

Also, a blessing allows us to draw close to our Gkids, for them to cleave to us, and to establish an intimate relationship with them. Another impact of speaking a blessing can be to change a worldly perspective on their lives into a Godly perspective. A blessing can give our Gkids God's glasses through which to view and evaluate their lives. Giving a blessing is a blessing!

In their book, Smalley and Trent identify 5 aspects of giving a blessing: 1) Meaningful touch; 2) Spoken message; 3) Attach high value to one blessed; 4) Picture a special future; 5) Active commitment to help fulfill the blessing.

For now, we will focus on the first two. First, meaningful touch. We all know touch will certainly be a part of our Gkids' lives. The question is from whom will they be receiving it. Experiencing positive touch from you is far better than other potential touch! Really meaningful touch is often during the 'bad' times. Jesus modeled this for us in Mark 1 by going to the extreme of touching a leper. In this Biblical account, Jesus was moved with compassion, stretched out His hand, and touched them. A simple touch when our Gkids are hurting can go a long way in comforting them.

Again we look to Jesus regarding touching. This time He touches children. In Mark 10 we read where Jesus asked that little ones be brought to Him so that He might touch them! Appropriate physical affection, especially during bad or leprous type moments, cannot be overstated. No one else may be reaching out to touch your Gkid during these times, but WE are to be the ones! And when we speak a blessing, we are to use healthy touch as well!

When bestowing a blessing with words, some of you may be thinking blessing with words might be too difficult, as we don't bless much anymore in our culture. Let's start with what you might think is small or easy and move from there. Think of something you are currently praying about regarding one of your Gkids. Now, all you have to do is add two words and replace their names with pronouns! That's it! Hopefully, you're gaining confidence that even you will be able to speak a blessing into the lives of your Gkids!

An example should help. Say your grandson, Mark, is going to attend church camp, and you're praying the following: 'Lord be with Mark at camp. Keep him safe and help him to draw closer to You.' First, you will bless them by telling them you are praying for them. After that, you can bless them by speaking that prayer with the minor changes, which are indicated in bold. Place your hand on their shoulder and say your blessing like this: '**May the** Lord be with **You at camp; may He** keep **You** safe; and **may He** help **You** to draw closer to **Him**.' You have just given them a blessing by saying what you were praying for them with some simple changes. Yes, you CAN speak a blessing into your Gkids' lives (and others too!).

Some of you may be thinking that this isn't much of a blessing. Let's compare it to Jacob as he blessed his Gkids and his son Joseph in Gen 48:15,16. This should be the 'Lord's Prayer' of blessings as it comes from one of the patriarchs. Here it is: *Then he blessed Joseph and said, "May the God before whom my fathers Abraham and Isaac walked faithfully, the God who has been my shepherd all my life to this day, the Angel who has delivered me from all harm—may he bless these boys. May they be called by my name and the names of my fathers Abraham and Isaac, and may they increase greatly on the earth."*

I believe you can do a much better blessing than this! Jacob merely talked to God about himself, blessed his Gkids by simply saying the word bless, wanted them to be called by his name, and

87

wanted them to multiply. I trust that now with a little practice, you will easily be able to place a unique and special blessing on each of your Gkids on a regular basis!

Another 'easy' way to bless is to use God's word as a blessing. You may want to write the Scripture before trying to speak it, as these Biblical blessings are powerful and can be a great blessing to your Gkids. The verses in Ephesians 1:17-19a are an example of ones you can quote as your state or write your blessing to them!

However, to give a relevant blessing, you have to be a student of the one being blessed. Know what your Gkids are involved in and are going through, and then address that circumstance specifically. For example, if one of them is involved in a competition or performance, speak to them words of encouragement regarding what they are doing.

With practice, you can look into their future for a blessing, but take care that you don't express 'hidden agendas' when blessing! For example, you may bless them regarding whom they will marry, but not by saying, 'May the Lord help you to marry well, because you're so irresponsible you'd never make it on your own!' No, speak the truth in love and stop at 'May the Lord help you to marry well!'

Also, consider their nature, strengths, and gifting when suggesting career opportunities that would be a good match for them. You may be charting a special future for them by giving them hope in a difficult world! A blessing also can be very informal. You can be walking with them to a game and simply put your arm around them and say, 'May the Lord help you to have a great attitude during this game, and may He help you to do your very best.' This simple blessing can change their whole approach to their upcoming game, helping them change their focus from winning to what God wants from them.

Whatever blessing you choose, say it in a voice that means it. You can be silly as a grandparent and that's a good thing, but you should be serious about spiritual things. So when blessing, stop, give eye contact, act like they are the only person in the whole world, touch them appropriately and speak God's blessing into their lives!

Leaving a legacy is not a choice as it will happen. BUT we have to intentionally choose to be and to bestow a blessing on our Gkids! This was God's instruction to Moses regarding giving a blessing to the people of Israel and is an excellent example of the type of blessing we can give:

"May the Lord bless you and keep you; may the Lord make His face to shine upon you and be gracious to you; may the Lord lift up His countenance upon you and give you peace." Numbers 6:24-26

ACTION PLAN – CHAPTER THIRTEEN

Write 3 – 5 specific ways in which you can be a blessing in your Gkids' lives.

Pick one of your Gkids you have been praying for and write that prayer as a blessing.

Practice speaking a blessing to your spouse or a close friend or even the mirror, but take time to practice bestowing a blessing with words!

CHAPTER FOURTEEN

Special or Spoiled

I once read a comment that went something like this: 'The reason that Gkids are spoiled is because nobody is willing to spank Grandma.' My wife would argue that in our case it should be that no one is willing to spank Papa. Our goal is not to take on the worldly advice to spoil them and then to give them back to the parents. No, we are to let them know they are special, but not spoil them. A general definition of impressing the hearts of our Gkids with the knowledge they are special would be something like this – 'Without undermining the wishes of the parents, making your Gkids feel valued and held in high esteem in ways that help them, not hurt them.' Similar to the use of our words, our actions are always to be helpful, not hurtful!

When trying to make our Gkids feel special without spoiling them, the goal is to be able to dote over them without disrespecting their parents! Remember, the parents are the conduit to your Gkids! Letting Gkids have their favorites is certainly part of making them feel special, but if their favorites are off-limits according to their parents, we must find some other way to do so.

One parent I talked to referred to their desire to keep sugar away from their kids, but the grandparents would sneak sugary treats to them. This did damage to their relationship with their parents and their kids. The parents were stuck in the middle and had trouble on both sides. We must try to avoid this. We are to communicate with the parents. If we don't like their answer, too bad! We took our first grandson to 'Old McDonalds' every time he came, and even though that's not part of his parents' scheduled eating habits for him, we made sure they are OK with us taking him there!

As grandparents, we have an irrational pride in our Gkids, which can easily result in spoiling. I was on a walk with my first baby grandson and asked two other hikers if they wanted to look at the cutest Gkid ever! They stated that all grandparents say that, but my response was, "Yeah, but the difference is that I'm the only one who's telling the truth!"

While doting over them, we must remember that we are NOT Santa Claus. They don't need to get everything they want. But we can be like Santa in that we can evaluate if they're being naughty or nice. We shouldn't overlook bad behavior. We can discipline and set boundaries while still making them feel special! Throughout Proverbs we are told that children require discipline. However, our correction should be done privately while spending the necessary time to make them understand what they had done wrong. But always remember, we still can do unique things, like one person said her grandparents did; they always snuck them crackers during Mass!

While the job of parents is to teach and correct, we grandparents can do fun things that make our Gkids feel special without being hurtful. Here are some things others have done that you might want to steal. We get to 'do it again Nana' over and over and over. Our presence and time give them the feeling that they truly are special and important! We can send them Youtubes of their interests or send articles or books. When we bring things to them in areas of their interest, it brings credibility to our interest in them when we give them a blessing! We can surprise them by picking them up for a surprise vacation or a day off from school. It can be as simple as having a huge bowl and giant spoon, so when they come over, they always have ice cream with those. Or it could be silly words like one grandparent who took the Gkids for donuts and always said, 'Make sure you don't eat the hole in the donut!'

Other activities include things like when my wife spends special time with our Gkids by reading books of a spiritual nature and singing Christian songs with them. Taking them to a Christian family camp provides spiritual impact and plenty of fun! We have committed to making sure the finances are taken care of regarding summer and winter Christian camps, as we have personally experienced the impact of camp on our lives. We can let them try stuff and explore their ideas, which helps build confidence and overcome fears. One person shared that her grandparents would make them breakfast in their camper! We could have their favorite foods or movies or take them to a game of their favorite athletic team. We can be silly by putting gummy worms in our noses, or letting them shoot spit wads through a straw at our glasses in a restaurant. Making them laugh helps impress their hearts, and reminds them that they are special to us! Also, we can show them that they are special with our words. Not just flattering words, but words using specific examples of positive, encouraging things they have done regarding their inner package. Like 'I noticed you helping Susie. You really are a good friend.' There are lots of ways to make our precious Gkids feel special!

A word of warning! Make sure you make them feel special equally! Each one of our Gkids is unique, so we can treat them somewhat differently. Some may be easier to interact with, but we must treat each one basically the same. Plus, it is very important to treat each different family of Gkids equally. This may be hard, but if we treat one set of Gkids differently than another set, bad results are almost guaranteed. I know of two siblings who don't talk to each other, which is primarily due to how differently 'Grandma' treated the Gkids in each family.

Another warning! Using money to try to make them feel special can easily be more hurtful than helpful. Question: Which is better? For the Gkids to have too much money or too little? I once overheard a well-off person at a restaurant share that the money he was given as a child was not good for him. Proverbs 30: 8, 9 is an appropriate prayer regarding this: *"Keep falsehood and lies far from me; give me neither poverty nor riches, but give me only my daily bread. Otherwise, I may have too much and disown You and say, 'Who is the Lord?' Or I may become poor and steal, and so dishonor the name of my God."*

Some of us don't have the finances to worry about giving our Gkids too much money, but we must never allow them to place a high value on money. For what does I Timothy 6:10 say is the root of ALL evil? The LOVE of money. We can be creative enough without having to depend on buying their love. Spending time with them with a cardboard box is often better than simply buying them some expensive toy! Many grandparents can afford to buy things which the parents may not want their kids to have. Remember, we should stay within the parents' financial plan for them. If parents don't want them to have it, they shouldn't have it even as a birthday present or at Christmas.

There are many potential benefits and lessons from money. An important one would be learning to earn money by working. I pay my Gkids well, but only in response to them having earned it! My wife and I have taken out a life insurance policy on each Gkid in case of a short-term tragedy and also as a long-term investment. We knew of a couple whose baby fell victim to SIDS. The funeral costs had to be borrowed and monthly payments had to be made. We vowed never to chance an event like this happening in our family; hence the life insurance.

A savings account can be started, and some money can be deposited every birthday encouraging your Gkids to develop a savings plan! One Grandparent gave a significant amount of money if their Gkid didn't have a ticket or accident the first two years they drove. Certainly money should not be a major part of our legacy, yet one Gkid shared how much she appreciated her grandparents who gave her spending money that allowed her to do some extra things her Mom couldn't afford! Money and Gkids have to meet the usual standard – has it been OK'd by their parents, and is it helpful not hurtful? Your most important gift is your gift of time and love!

But you can spoil your Gkids' parents! We tend to get so caught up in Gkids that we don't even notice our kids anymore. We made that mistake with my daughter and son where they both felt the Gkids took us away from them. Now when we visit them, we make sure to give our kids special attention as well! With your kids, money can be used wisely to help them set up a college fund or help send them on a special vacation. Also, you can spoil them by volunteering to take the Gkids for a free night of babysitting. Or get your kids a night at a hotel or gift certificate to their favorite restaurant! Don't forget to spoil your kids a little, while also making them feel special as well!

To make our Gkids feel special, we must do things for them which we would not do for anyone else! A good summary might be this – 'we don't want to spoil our Gkids, but we are trying to make them feel as special as we can. Special to us and special to God.'

ACTION PLAN – CHAPTER FOURTEEN

Do you think you've been guilty of spoiling your Gkids? How can you adjust that to make them feel special without spoiling them?

List a few ways you will use money and time to create a special feeling within the hearts of your Gkids.

Write down some ways you can spoil your kids.

CHAPTER FIFTEEN

Undermining or Uplifting

When I was growing up, my Dad had 3 categories when someone said something negative about him. He put their comment in its proper category, and his response was predetermined! His categories were: 1) If their statement was true, he would change whatever he had done. 2) If it wasn't true, there was nothing he could do about it. And 3) If the comment was spoken by someone whom he didn't respect, then he chose to ignore it. I took these on and still use them today. This concept can effectively be applied to our role as grandparents as well!

Our goal is to always uplift our kids and Gkids, not undermine them. But sadly, there are many stories where relationships were damaged, as words spoken when not wanted caused massive conflict within a family. To counteract this, we are now going to utilize 3 categories or boxes. The goal is to create less tension in the family, and make it much easier to intentionally control your responses!

First, how many readers would be willing to admit they have control issues? If you were a micro-managing parent, it can worsen as a grandparent. This may be hard for you controlling types, but it is very important to get a handle on this issue. Now with Gkids, it's indeed time for us to let go of the need to control and let God intervene in their lives!

Also, we all had differing parenting styles, and our kids will as well. It is important to remember that your child's spouse certainly does not have your child's nature. Plus, the odds are that they were raised in a completely different family environment than your child, and their parenting will reflect their reaction to the family style they lived in. If it isn't already too late, you may want to consider sitting down with your new in-law's parents. The goal being to find out as much as you can about how your new in-law was raised, family traditions, and any other information which would help you know them better. For example, we didn't know that our daughter-in-law's family didn't make a big deal out of birthdays like we did. We had to figure that one out the hard way!

Your new son or daughter-in-law may have made definite commitments while being raised as to what they would or would not do as a parent. Yet, you are completely unaware of those commitments. I'm pretty sure my in-laws weren't too happy when I gave my totally white-haired 3-year-old son a buzz cut when the style was fairly long hair. He looked like a balding 3-year old!

The new family's habits, reactions, and preferences may be quite different than 'how you think it SHOULD be done.' You know, the way you did parenting! Advice offered which has not been asked for can easily undermine important relationships!

Now the categories, which I'll label Box 1, Box 2, and Box 3. My creativity is amazing, eh? Each box represents an action by our kids or Gkids, and then we predetermine our response depending on which box the action falls in.

Box 1: We'll do the predetermined response first. When you decide that something falls in this category, you are NOT to say anything! Zip it, put your top lip against the bottom one and keep it there, shut up – whatever works! The way to react to Box 1 events is for that *golden* silence!

So, what are the actions, words, or events which belong in Box 1? **Personal preferences.** Our wishes here are important, and you might even win the battle if you choose to engage here. But this is a category in which you have to trust God to win the war and simply (maybe not so simply) BE QUIET! If you do open your mouth at this time, it must be to God alone! Examples of personal preferences are pacifiers, thumb-sucking, blankie or no blankie, family dinner or dinner in front of the TV, clothing or hair issues and more. Are these preferences worth potentially damaging your relationship with your Gkids or kids?

Remember when your parents interfered with your family concerning issues like this. How did you like it? So when there is a concern and you place it in box 1, what are you to do? Talk about it ONLY to God!!! My wife and I know of a grandmother who didn't like her grandson's haircut, and brought him home from preschool with a new haircut – not good! In this box we need to **ACCEPT** the preferences of others. We may never know what our acceptance and silence did to avoid harsh or offensive words which we can never take back!

One couple responded to this section of my seminar by stating that by adopting the principle of Box 1, it really changed their lives! Their daughter had gotten a divorce, and she and her new baby lived with them. They said this principle helped them, 'Don't go there!' and they believe that allowed them to avoid many negative interactions.

Box 3 – I'm skipping to Box 3 as it is like Box 1 in that we should have no choice regarding our response to actions we place in these two boxes. Whereas in Box 1 we are to be silent, in this box we must **ACT!** This is crisis intervention time. Prayerfully this will never happen to you. In Box 3, your Gkid is definitely in peril because of their parents being involved with things like abuse, drugs, or run-ins with the law.

I am intimately aware of a family in which the death of their Gkid's parent caused the grandparents to act. Not only did they take in their 9-year old granddaughter, she had special needs and required significant attention. To say their lives changed is a complete understatement as they have been responsible for her for 20 years, and she is still living with them. To verify the above details I contacted these grandparents. And as we were talking, they were taking her to the hospital.

In this case, you may be their only hope. However, you should always allow your Gkid to experience the natural consequences of their actions and not bail them out. But when the parent is the cause, you must step in. Again, prayer is first, and then seek professional help and utilize community resources. In these situations, there IS a price to pay and it may be a high price, but you must ACT! God knew this was going to happen and has prepared you, with His help, to be just the right grandparent for the job!

Simone Biles' upbringing is a great example of a Box 3 event. If you find yourself taking in your Gkids and lose confidence, consider her and what her grandparents did! There's always hope!

Box 2 – These are the toughies! In this box are issues of values, discipline, traditions, and faith! Something of importance is going on, but you haven't been asked for input. Yet you feel the need to do or say something. The first step when Box 2 actions occur is similar to Box 1. Don't say anything immediately and take the time to pray. Before you do anything, ask other Christ-followers whom you trust for wisdom regarding what should be done. Their advice can help you maintain your objectivity thru the process as when emotions take over, bad things can easily happen. I was intending on confronting an in-law, but after sharing it with good friends, I took their advice and remained silent!

Through prayer, ask God as to how you should respond, and ALWAYS remember – God can speak loudly without using words. His communication to us does not depend on words alone, as He loudly revealed His majesty in creation. Jesus often taught, yet He also conveyed His love without many words. If you ever owned a red-letter edition Bible, the first part of each gospel is filled with red letters indicating when Jesus was speaking. However, the last chapters of the gospels have very few words in red. Yet during those latter chapters when Jesus was mostly silent, God spoke louder than when Jesus spoke a lot! Always trust Him to be impacting your Gkids' lives even when He leads you to remain silent.

When you choose to speak in response to Box 2 occurrences, are you willing to communicate and actually hear a response which doesn't seem true to you? And then allow them to continue the same course of action without your interference? Is it OK for them to say no? Do we love and value our traditions or other important issues more than our relationship with our kids?

Addressing the situation may be the best alternative, but handle that conversation with extreme caution! So when you choose to overtly involve yourself with the issue, here are some suggestions. Make sure it's done in private, and be sure to keep it away from the Gkids. It is also very important in these situations that your words give grace to the hearer.

A great way to begin is to utilize questions. Whenever Jesus ran into a conflict, He used questions to respond. Sometimes that was all that needed to be said. A good general question is: 'and how's that working for you?' Ask humbly, not with an attitude! Another method is to tell stories or life experiences that make your point. Jesus called His stories with a point, parables. Author George

MacDonald wrote stories filled with life lessons, which were enough to influence CS Lewis for Christ. Become a good storyteller! And if you can start your conversation with 'this is what God taught me when I was your age and going thru a similar situation,' you are now simply sharing one of your life experiences, not forcing your ideas on them!

Compromise may be the final answer. Although your way may be best, half way may be the maximum. For example: your kids are not taking your Gkids to church. You want them to, but they won't, so you offer to take them when you can and continue to model your faith when the Gkids are at your home. So when situations arise in Box 2, pray first, seek help from wise Christ-following friends, and maybe you will be led to **ADDRESS** your predicament and maybe you won't. But always pray!!!

To review: If the event falls in Box 1, we are silent and great prayer warriors. In Box 3, we must intervene regardless of the cost. And that middle Box 2 is where a wise decision must be made, and we must follow God's leading. Box 1 – Accept; Box 2 – Address?; Box 3 – Act!

ACTION PLAN – CHAPTER FIFTEEN

If you are doing this action plan with others, talk about the different habits and traditions your new in-laws brought into your family. Or if doing this alone, list those differences.

Write down examples of issues you believe should be placed in Box 1, Personal Preferences.

Which area of Box 2 do you believe will be the most challenging with your kids' families? Traditions, issues of faith, values, or discipline. What can you proactively do to alleviate potential conflict?

Say a prayer of commitment to God that you will Act if anything happens in Box 3.

CHAPTER SIXTEEN

Divorce

Divorce is something that can happen in any generation within families; to the grandparents, the parents, or even the Gkids. When it happens in a family, the issues become challenges, but those challenges CAN be overcome! It will take considerable energy and effort, but divorce provides unique and important opportunities to minister to our Gkids. However, divorce discussions come with a warning – CAUTION: fragile or sensitive material inside! While reading, remember that it is all written with the intent of helping the Gkids navigate through a difficult time – so here we go!

No matter who is divorced, even if it's the grandparents themselves, grandparents still are central to how this plays out in the life of the Gkids. In a divorce, your son or daughter is at least a part of the problem. Your wisdom and modeling of Godly behavior are vital to the eventual adjustments your Gkids have to make to their new environment. And remember, you will be seeing your ex-in-law at little league games, performances, graduations, and marriages so don't burn any bridges, no matter how much fuel they've given you!

During the divorce process, grandparents have to remain objective, and we often need help from someone not directly involved to give us the correct perspective. A few thoughts: 1) Don't add your pain to the pain your Gkid is experiencing! You should have the most maturity and your Gkid the least, so act like it! When Godly wisdom isn't present during a divorce, damage ensues and most of it lands on the Gkids.

2) Don't go through this alone. God will be there for you, but friends will help as well! Use them as a sounding board and as an encourager while you struggle through the process. You may even need to consider talking with a Christian counselor for help during this time.

3) The protective nature every parent has will be activated when your child is less at fault for the issues that caused the divorce. But even if that is true, your protective nature cannot run wild and wreak havoc. It must be recognized and controlled! Or the opposite may be true and your child is the major cause of the divorce. Now disappointment and possible depression have to be dealt with. This will be a very emotional time, and you have to be prepared to be as objective as possible. One way to prepare for this and any other tragic event is to present all of your children to the Lord as His, not yours. You may have done this once, or a thousand times, but right now, pray the following and commit each of your kids into the hands of their loving heavenly Father!

"Almighty God, thank You for the gift of my children. As Samuel's Mother gave him to the Lord, I give my children to You for all the days of their lives. Help me to trust completely in Your loving care of them – they are Yours."

When the agonizing process is over and the divorce is final, we as grandparents must help in the healing process. In my experience with divorce issues, one of the biggest factors in the difficulties which eventually present themselves is the 'lack of normalcy.' For long-term healing and success,

I believe the entire family must strive to become as 'normal' as possible as soon as possible. This is especially true if there is a remarriage and new Gkids enter your family. God is not surprised. This new family is now His plan A, and I don't believe He has the words 'dysfunctional family' or 'step kids' in His vocabulary.

As best as we can, we must seek to establish normal relationships with the new family unit. When words like 'birth parent,' 'not really my grandparent', 'you don't have any right to . . .' are being heard, we are now in box 3. Someone has to intervene to help get the entire family back on track. It will be harder in the short run, but much better in the long run.

Someone close to me divorced and remarried with both parties having children in the 8 to 15-year-old range. The birth parent took the responsibility for their respective kids and they never tried to be a normal family. The grandparents on each side also didn't really get involved with their new Gkids. That was over 30 years ago and none of them are very close today. Making every effort, though difficult, to be a 'normal' family can go a long way in healing AND in preventing major issues in the future!

When divorce happens, the grandparents surely need to reflect the Holy Spirit in helping the Gkids turn their fears into a faith that God WILL take them through this! Their fears are very real to them. Where am I going to live? What school am I going to go to? Will I like my new family? What if they don't like me? Will I have to get all new friends? Where is God in all of this? Helping them through these fears demonstrates why this is such an extremely important time for you to come alongside your Gkids and your kids. They will need your love and support then more than ever!

Ironically while editing this chapter, my good friend texted me about his divorced son and his Gkids. He texted this, 'This is the first divorce we have ever dealt with, and the fall out is something else.' Divorce happens far too often, and we must be prepared to be used by God to help in any way we can! This topic deserves a lot of attention as this has just scratched the surface – maybe my next book?

ACTION PLAN – CHAPTER SIXTEEN

In what ways can you show compassionate leadership if there is a divorce in your family, or how could you help a friend's family going through one?

Write down the names of your close friends whom you can go to during challenging times within your family.

Although attempting to be a normal family within divorce is hard, write down some long-term benefits by doing so.

CHAPTER SEVENTEEN

Long-Distance Grandparenting

Let's begin with the most important thing about this topic: to make sure your Gkids KNOW that they are always on your mind! How you do this can vary greatly, but you must be a regular presence in their lives and your actions must convey that they are just as special to you far away as they would be if they lived next door!

Fortunately for those grandparents who find themselves in this situation, now is the best time in all of history to be distanced from your Gkids. Technology enables connection in a way never before available. Although your Gkids are far away, God's purpose doesn't change regarding your role as a grandparent. You can no longer be what I used to call myself: 'roadkill on the technological super-highway!' Technology may never become your close friend, but when it comes to your Gkids, it can't be your enemy either!

Some examples: Texting is something kids can't stay away from. Even when they get texts at school, they will risk getting in trouble to read them. Zoom is very fun and pretty easy! Send photos via technology or even hard copies through the mail. They love photos! These methods of communicating are not that hard to learn. I know texting with big old fingers can be tough, but you can use voice messaging. Just be SURE to proofread before you send. We have a men's group called M6, and I texted my pastor friend by speaking, 'Are you going to M6 tonight?' However, the voice recognition person wrote this out as, 'Are you going to have sex tonight?' Again, proofread those voice texts before sending!

All of you probably can email. You can do that individually, or even have a group email which includes all your Gkids! Whatever technology you choose, it doesn't have to be fancy. You reaching out serves as a reminder to them that they are on your mind. And you never know what it might mean to them on any given day! Whether or not your teenage Gkids are close or distant, a Friday and Saturday night text at 6 p.m. simply stating, 'Be Good!' could make a big difference in what decisions they might make that night!

An old-school phone call or sending a card IS still very appropriate and maybe even more special now because it doesn't happen as often. Don't feel like you have to abandon these forms of communication. When your Gkids are young, the phone calls may be a bit difficult, but they still send the message that you want to be part of their lives! As they grow older and you are a good student of your Gkids, you will have lots to talk about. Remember to ask appropriate questions to keep them talking. Try to avoid yes and no questions. Use open-ended ones on topics you already KNOW they are interested in!

Take full advantage of times when you do get to visit with them. By that I mean stretch a one-week visit into three months. How you ask – well, before you're physically together, do some pre-planning. Talk to them about things they would like to do, and special foods they would love you to have or make. Create thought-provoking anticipation far before the trip actually happens. After all, anticipation is said to be half the fun!

And then after the trip, make reference to it in future phone calls or texts. A one-week visit can keep you connected much longer by pre-planning with them before your trip, and after it by talking about the memories you made while together!

Here are two examples of long-distance relationships. The first is a woman who has Gkids about 100 miles away. She lives in an area where people come to vacation, and she complained about how the Gkids only contact her when they are in the area vacationing. Otherwise, she shared, there was little to no contact. Because she was doing me a favor at the time, I didn't do anything, but I wanted to confront her and tell her that SHE should be the one initiating regular contact to demonstrate HER interest in them. Hopefully, God touches her heart and she now does that!

That very same day I talked with a girl who had two sets of grandparents. One was local and the other about 300 miles away. She shared about the differing relationship she had with each, and I responded about the one she didn't know well with, "It's hard when they are far away." She responded, "No, those are the ones who live nearby. I'm much closer to the ones who live far away!" This confirmed to me that long-distance grandparenting does work!

Whatever contact you make, consistency is the key. It doesn't have to be every day, but there cannot be large time gaps between the times you re-establish your presence in their lives. It doesn't matter if you're close or far away, your consistency brings the certainty to them that their grandparents really care about them, which brings comfort! There WILL be times in your Gkids' lives when things get hard and nobody seems to care, but your actions will shout to them – Grandma and Grandpa do!!!

ACTION PLAN – CHAPTER SEVENTEEN

List specific ways you can have your Gkids know that they are always on your mind, whether they are a long distance away or close by.

Write ways you can stretch a short visit into something that lasts much longer.

What does consistent contact mean in your relationship with your Gkids?

CHAPTER EIGHTEEN

Miscellaneous Topics

Grandparenting Teens: One age group that seems especially challenging for grandparents to engage with is teenagers. I've worked with teens most of my life and although they seem scary and hard to reach, they are not! However, even in good family environments, your Gkids probably will be in some type of adversarial relationship with their parents. This gives you the opportunity to fill the role of the one (and maybe the only one) they can go to and share things with, as you reflect the Holy Spirit in their lives – their comforter. Remember what the girl shared in the chapter on our legacy? One set of grandparents was approachable and one was not. Your goal is to be the Godly non-judgmental grandparent your Gkids will go to during hard times in their lives.

Yes, teens are sensitive and insecure, so be careful with your words. There will be many times you will need to give them grace with your words, or be silent. They also will probably give you a ton of opportunities to disagree with their lifestyles and preferences, but as their grandparent, you should be the steady, patient, wise, and accepting one!

I've worked with so many troubled teens who have become very successful adults. Recently at a counselors' luncheon an ex-student, now a counselor and happily married, reminded me of when she was my counselee and got expelled from high school for a litany of reasons. Eventually, she went to a continuation high school. But, she made it! There is ALWAYS hope.

Do NOT run from teens! Things may not go perfectly, but you are NOT out of touch with them, and you DON'T have to be like them or know their terminology for them to want to be with you. There is a God-given connection between grandparents and their Gkids, which remains even during the teen years.

Practically speaking, teenagers like food, things to do, and money! Use that knowledge to plan activities or be involved in what they are involved with, even if that means watching them play games on their phone. Take them to eat or go to places or events they like. When it seems appropriate, give them a bit of money and go shopping for something they want. Be careful not to over invade their space and their lives, but don't stay away from them thinking you're not wanted.

Even though teens tend to choose spending time with friends over relatives, yet somewhat surprisingly, your teenage Gkids really value the love of family! Remember, love never fails. You may think some of your time with them was a waste or a failure, but your love will never go unnoticed or unappreciated. Do all you can to model God's love and make sure your love with your teen Gkids is unconditional. The greatest gift you can give them is the gift of your time and your love!

Living together with your Gkids. It is estimated that across the United States, more than 13 million children are currently living in homes with their grandparents. In many of these cases, there is not a parent in the home. So much goes into this, as now the grandparent is both the parent and grandparent, or they have to balance living with their child again as well as Gkids. A tough place to be. This certainly was not your Plan A when you were rocking your infant children and thinking about their future. I'm sure you didn't think, 'Let's see, I think I'll be taking care of your children someday!'

These instances are either temporary or long-term. If temporary, consider it as an extended visit or vacation with them. However, if it is long-term, that's another story! But in these cases, you may be their only hope! As with divorce, normalcy is the goal, so seek that within the dysfunction!

Whether temporary or long term, this IS now their family and they're not just visiting. God is very aware that this was going to happen, and your situation is now His plan A and should be yours as well. There is brokenness requiring validation and validation requires you.

Make every effort to team with God to validate their circumstances and always let them know that this is the #1 thing God has called you to do, and that you are excited about the opportunity!

I had a student who was a long term live in with her grandparents. Though difficult for all of them, she was highly successful and earned a full-ride scholarship to a prominent California university. To have one's Gkids live with them is a special privilege given by God to qualified grandparents. If it happens to you, seek all the help you can get within your church and community. There are resources which can assist you in a number of ways. Don't shy away from accepting help, as going it alone will make things even more challenging. God created us to live in community, and so many people are more than willing to help. Let them!

Babysitting. When asked to babysit, the goal is for your Gkids to want to be at Grandma and Grandpa's house! If you've been their student and observed them closely, then babysitting will be a joy as you have their favorites and are genuinely interested in what's important to them! When issues of discipline arise, you should have already talked to your kids about this – remember Pre-framing?

Plus, you're often better off acting as an accountant rather than an enforcer when it comes to babysitting. By that I mean the pen is mightier than the sword! Rather than arguing about what they should be doing, tell your Gkids you're writing their behaviors down and that their parents (pre-agreed upon) will take care of whatever issues arise. No corporal punishment is recommended! Time-outs and taking things are all right, but let your kids take care of other forms of discipline. Plan ahead for activities and projects that you can do together. They may watch TV shows that are a bit different than you're normal style, but you can handle a few kids' shows, can't you! Babysitting should be great fun and something that both parties look forward to!

As I am writing this, my son and daughter-in-law are talking to my wife, because we will be babysitting their three kids for the next four days – time for me to practice what I preach!

ACTION PLAN – CHAPTER EIGHTEEN

List ways in which you plan to interact with your teenage Gkids in activities they like to do.

If any of your Gkids are currently living with you, write down a time you will meet with them and share how important it is to you that God put them in your life at this time.

When you babysit, what are the unique things you do that are special to them? Are there other things you could be doing? Write those down as well.

CHAPTER NINETEEN

A Difficult Challenge
And Being On The Same Page

When teaching a grandparenting class at a local prison, one inmate shared that during his teens, his Grandma planted a spiritual seed in him which he tried hard to destroy. He couldn't. And it wasn't until he landed in prison that the seed began to grow and he gave his life to Christ. I'll repeat it again. There's always hope, so never give up!

Grandparenting is filled with great joys and wonderful experiences, but – sadly, there is this but – but difficult challenges also arise. The specifics of these challenges vary within individual families and need to be addressed on that basis. Though I will be sharing some general thoughts, my contact information is at the back of the book to enable us to communicate directly about your unique situation. Please contact me, and I'll get back to you!

Probably the most difficult challenge for those of us who prioritize being a Godly grandparent is when a spiritual division arises within one's family. The range could be from the extreme of not being allowed to communicate or see your Gkids at all, to smaller differences in regards to issues of faith. Whatever level you might be experiencing, spiritual concerns genuinely hurt Godly grandparents' hearts!

What to do? Be consistent! You may not be able to be consistent with your presence, but you can be with your love, concern, and involvement. A good friend of mine has had the extreme happen, and his daughter will not allow him to have any contact with her or his Gkids. So he decided to build a future treasure chest for all of them. Within that chest he will put notes, holiday cards, holiday gifts (probably all will be money), and more. The hope – never lose hope – being that someday there will be some form of reconciliation. When that happens, he will give his daughter and Gkids their treasure chests! Rather than just being happy they can communicate and say, 'I missed you,' he will have proof of his consistent love for them over the years.

What a day that will be when each note and card are read. Much joy will ensue when they accept the gifts he couldn't give them at the time, but saved for them for this day. Then they will fully realize that Grandpa truly loved and cared for them throughout their years of physical separation!

If this type of relationship happens in your family, I encourage you to do the same! Words of sorrow for the time apart are one thing, but physical evidence of that sorrow will go a long way in setting a strong foundation for your future relationship. For many of us, this is how God pursued us. When we refused to respond to His call on our lives, He put people, events, or words in our path until the point we finally committed our lives to Him. As we look back, the evidence of His continued love for us makes our relationship with Him even more precious!

Whatever level of challenge you face in this area, do not retreat into a world of depressed noth-ingness. Have hope! Pray! Save any letters, notes, and cards you would have given them, so that you can give them all of those at a later date! Remember that God CAN and WILL speak loudly to them without your words! When you get a chance to get together, come as a gentle lamb not a raging bull! And do all things with love – you are after their hearts not their minds or bodies – so even if you are in the right and have all the reasonable arguments on your side, without love that is nothing! Again, please contact me directly so we can talk specifically about your issues.

Another challenge in grandparenting is for married grandparents. Sometimes we're not on the same page. You might say, 'Oh wait, as Christ-followers, we are now one!' Well, I'm married, and I know oneness only goes so far! And it doesn't always extend to the many decisions which need to be made in the grandparenting arena.

Remember how you or your kids used to ask Mom for certain things and Dad for others! As grand-parents, we should be wise to that game. The goal here is not to be or become one in all areas, but to act as one! This requires communication. It requires the pre-planning and pre-framing de-scribed in Chapter 10. It also requires the patient responding as outlined in Chapter 14. Reactions not well thought out could easily put the two of you at odds with each other and send a mixed message to your Gkids. And like other aspects of marriage, it requires proactive and intentional compromise!

It seems like a lot of requirements for getting on the same page, but being there is absolutely worth it. To have a unified presence in your Gkids' lives is a worthy goal. This still allows room for one grandparent to have a special relationship with one of your Gkids, as one of you may have developed private areas of trust. But it should exclude the 'don't tell Grandma' type thing, as it is obvious you are hiding something they wouldn't agree with. Plus, little kids aren't good at keeping secrets and when Grandma finds out . . . well, you know how that plays out!

If you're a couple and it hasn't already been part of your Action Plan in a previous chapter, make sure you communicate directly about being on the same page at the end of this chapter!

ACTION PLAN – CHAPTER NINETEEN

If you aren't able to be with any of your Gkids, commit to starting a treasure chest of cards/gifts/notes. You can even backdate some of them if your separation has gone on for a while. This is very important!

If you are a married couple, pray together and decide the best way to be on the same page with each other. Discuss ways you have not done that in the past and how you can improve.

CHAPTER TWENTY

Encouragement And A Closing Blessing

As we end our time together, I want to thank you for reading this book, but my real desire is that you make Godly grandparenting a top priority in your life. Yes, knowledge is power, but the application of information is where real change happens. I trust you have been Romans 12:2'd and you have renewed your mind regarding your current role in the lives of your precious Gkids!

Success is found in the effort, yet sometimes we even get to experience actual results in the present! While relying on God, humbly approach each encounter with your Gkids as a gift from the God who has a plan for you, has prepared you, and is partnering with you for His purpose!

Earlier we referenced Phillipians 3:13, 14 which states, *but this one thing I do, forgetting what lies behind and reaching forward to what lies ahead, I press on toward the* **goal** *for the* **prize** *of the upward* **call** *of God in Christ Jesus.* As you consider your past as a parent and/or grandparent, you might feel a bit guilty for some of the things you have or haven't done. I find these verses very helpful at those times – my desire is to reach forward to what lies ahead.

Let me break down the verse emphasizing key words within the verse: 1) Goal: Our goal is for our Gkids to learn to fear the Lord all the days they live on earth. 2) Prize: The prize would be our Gkids choosing Jesus and loving the Lord similar to what the ceramic illustration demonstrated. And 3) Call: God's call on our lives as grandparents is for us to become the special, perfect Godly grandparent He designed us to be! Live out your call; seek the goal; and pray for the prize!

I'll close with two blessings. The first is a reminder of God's blessing to Israel found in Numbers 6:24-26 which we wrote at the end of the chapter on blessings:

May the Lord bless you and keep you;

May the Lord make His face shine upon you and be gracious unto you;

May the Lord lift up His countenance upon you, and may He give you peace!

AND MY BLESSING TO YOU:

May the Lord increase your faith in Him as you grow in the confidence that

you are in the exact place He has planned for you.

May the Lord give you hope for today and for tomorrow regarding the lives of your Gkids.

May the Lord grow your love for Him, and may He grant you multiple ways

you can show your love to your Gkids and impress their hearts.

And may the Lord partner with you as you intentionally and proactively

touch the hearts of each of your Gkids!

FINAL ACTION PLAN

List as many ways as you can regarding how you are going to be a more proactive and intentional Godly grandparent. (Then DO them!)

Appendix: Grandparenting Guidelines

These guidelines are designed to give you a very specific direction for grandparenting each of your individual Gkids. You will create one for each one of them, and some grandparents have chosen to do the same one for each Gkid. Others do a completely different one for each, while others had similar ones for every Gkid with minor changes.

There are three major goals for this project:

To give you specific direction as you Godly grandparent them.
To have the guidelines put up in their room as a reminder of the goals you have for them.
To be in their possession for the rest of their lives. A long-term result might be this: You are in heaven and your Gkid is not doing well. They are looking through their old stuff and run across the guideline you gave them. After reading it, they realize they are no way near what you wanted for them, and they commit to changing their life right there – what a joy that would be.

Here is a sample guideline for you to view what the final product looks like. Also, I've shared some sample goals various grandparents have used previously.

As your Namma and Papa,

we love you so much that we are promising before God to

intentionally impress upon your heart:

That you be humble, have a contrite spirit, tremble at God's word, and obey Him.

That you become in awe of Creator God

For you to consider others as more important than yourself

To be a mighty warrior of God

For you to be a man of your word

That your life is filled with Godly wisdom

For you to be sensitive to the needs of the brokenhearted

That music becomes your instrument to worship God and draw close to Him

Utilize any of the following or create your own unique goals for your Grandparenting Guide.

To be in awe of Creator God

That you consider others as more important than yourself

For you to always honor your parents

To exhibit the Fruit of the Spirit

That you recognize your spiritual gifting

For you to always follow through on your commitments

To know that you are important to us

That you make wise Godly choices

For you to always do unto others as you would have them do unto you

To pray and know that you are prayed for

That you are kind to people, animals, and the elderly

For you to always have a strong work ethic

To know your value and who you are in Christ

That you know God loves you unconditionally

For you to always know it's OK to be different

To build others up and not tear them down

That you know it's OK to be sad; it won't be like this forever

When creating the guidelines, have more spiritual goals than secular ones, and keep the total number under 10. That way I can use a big enough font to be readable when the guidelines are hanging on their bedroom walls. You will need to send or email me the goals, the name your Gkids call you, and their names. I will then type the final copy and send them to you on nice paper. Then you are to put them in a nice frame and give them to your Gkids.

If you pre-frame any possible problems with your kids, make sure you check with them first before distributing the framed guidelines. Then each year, possibly for dinner on their spiritual birthday, you should get together with each Gkid and check how YOU are doing in regards to the goals you had set for yourself.

After they give their feedback on you, a logical question you might ask would be, 'How are you doing with the guidelines?' Ideally, you will be able to have a deep two-way discussion about how both of you are doing.

I consider these guidelines to be a very important long-term benefit from you reading this book and trust you will prayerfully consider doing this!

About the Author

Larry has been married to Linda for over 51 years
and is the proud parent of two and Papa of five.
His career was as a counselor, teacher, and coach
at both public and Christian schools. He is currently Board Chairman for Fellowship of Christian
Athletes and Coaches Team International, which
brought him to China and North Korea doing
basketball ministry. He's been a speaker at various
men's and teen' retreats and has written a daily
devotional blog titled God2me for over 10 years. He
has presented the information in this book as a semi-

nar for 8 years primarily near his Central California Coast home and in various states. Currently,
he is retired; does life coaching; and pursues ministry in multiple ways.

His passion for sharing about Godly grandparenting resulted from Linda and him mentoring at a
parenting conference and realizing how much more they could have done spiritually as parents.
With his kids married and with children of their own, he and his wife decided to then focus on
grandparenting.

Contact Larry at hoek4@charter.net

Made in the USA
Monee, IL
10 June 2022

97732033R00077